43-7

318

Communism
and
the New Left

WHAT THEY'RE UP TO NOW

Communism and the New Left

WHAT THEY'RE UP TO NOW

BOOKS by U.S.NEWS & WORLD REPORT
A division of U.S.News & World Report, Inc.

WASHINGTON, D.C.

1969

34059

Contents

List of Illustrations

Introduction

There is considerable confusion in the United States about the different groups which make up the far left, old and new. This is due to a number of factors.

First there is the Communist Party-U.S.A., ever-loyal to Soviet Russia. This aged party realizes it cannot survive as a powerful influence unless it enters into the stream of the younger forces of the so-called "New Left." Hence its members may be found in the ranks of Students for a Democratic Society (SDS), one of the major groups of the New Left.

However, most youthful members of the New Left consider the Russians and their American followers to be "square" and "old hat"—products of a Soviet society which has gone soft and "bourgeois," not so different, in their opinion, from the United States.

The radical students themselves—described by one professor as "the spoiled children of the consumer society"—are another source of seeming contradiction. They have contempt for the urban, industrialized society, with its congestion and pollution, which gave them a world of plenty but left them, they say, spiritually impoverished. Looking for new gods, they turn to men like Mao Tse-tung, Che Guevara, and Fidel Castro—revolutionary figures who advocate guerrilla warfare. They may call themselves Marxists or communists, but they must be distinguished from Communists with a capital "C," members of the official U.S. party.

To complicate the picture further, we have two separate worlds among the Marxist left—one white, the other black. This separation is the will of young black radicals who seek to invert the original aim of Negroes to integrate into white society and who now advocate the kind of segregation that recalls the discredited positions of their white foes in the South of the United States and of Africa. Yet the revolutionary blacks have something in common with the radical whites—an addiction to communism (with a small "c"), to violence, and to guerrilla warfare.

Another point to be kept in mind is the fact that the far left does not have a border which fixes a limit between the campus and the rest of the country. The movement flows between the schools and the communities of the cities and towns. And it involves not only young people going to school but also older people who left school long ago or never went there. We are witnessing both an academic revolt and a political revolt—on-campus and off-campus—in search of a new university and a new society.

This book seeks to arrange these diverse elements of the far left into some order to provide an overall view of the forces which are creating turmoil in the United States today. Condensed outlines of the principal components of the far left will be found in chapters one and five. Documents in which leading groups describe their plans to destroy the present system in the United States will be found in the appendix.

Chapter One

The American Left: Old and New

Not since the depression of the 1930s has the United States seen so much activity by individuals and groups preaching Marxism, communism, and revolution. On campuses, on streetcorners, during mass demonstrations, speakers proclaim their determination to overthrow the capitalist system.

After years of steady decline in membership and influence, the Communist Party-U.S.A. is reviving. Its leaders are regular visitors to college campuses, where they expound the party line to student audiences. Party members are welcomed into the ranks of the antiwar movement and into some civil rights groups. And 1968 saw the party return openly to politics with a presidential ticket under the party banner for the first time since 1940.

The Communist Party is no longer alone on the far left. Some groups, formed after the Soviet-Chinese split in the world communist movement, violently reject the Moscow-oriented Communist Party-U.S.A. Others are the products of a new generation born after World War II. They are the youthful militants of the New Left.

It is the New Left that is most often in the spotlight today. Its members often are among the leaders of antiwar demonstrations and campus disruptions. The New Left has turned parts of the

Eight Major Components
of the Far Left

I. Students for a Democratic Society (SDS)
   (a) Revolutionary Youth Movement I (RYM I) (The Weatherman)
   (b) Progressive Labor Party—Worker-Student Alliance (PLP)
   (c) Revolutionary Youth Movement II (RYM II)
   (d) Trotskyite groups:
      (1) Young Socialist Alliance (YSA)
      (2) Youth Against War and Fascism
      (3) Johnson-Forrest Group
      (4) Sparticist League
   (e) Communist Party-USA (CP-USA) and its youth group, the DuBois Clubs of America
   (f) Independents (radicals who oppose the war and the establishment but do not endorse revolution)
II. Black Panther Party (BPP)
III. Student National Coordinating Committee (SNCC)
IV. Black Student Unions (BSU)
V. Revolutionary Action Movement (RAM)
VI. Republic of New Africa (RNA)
VII. Youth International Party (Yippies)
VIII. Freelancers: David Dellinger of National Mobilization Committee to End the War in Vietnam; Staughton Lynd of the Union of Organizers; Herbert Marcuse of University of California at San Diego; an estimated 100 militant black groups such as the Nation of Islam; Ramparts magazine; The Guardian.

Negro civil rights movement away from nonviolence and toward Black Power, and it is in the forefront of the latest attempt to instill Marxist ideas into the American labor movement.

What are the differences between the Old and New Left? What do they hope to accomplish? What are their tactics? How successful have they been?

Old or New, the groups of the far left share the same long-range goal: overthrow of the capitalist system in America. But they differ on how they would achieve this aim and on what would follow.

The Communist Party preaches the current Soviet line of peaceful coexistence. Gus Hall, the Communist Party's top official, unlike Nikita Khrushchev, does not say that our grandchildren will live under communism. He tells audiences that someday socialism will replace capitalism. He emphasizes that the change will come from within by peaceful means, not from the Soviet Union or any other foreign power. "U.S. socialism will be clearly marked, 'Made in U.S.A.,'" says Hall.

The future socialist America, as pictured by the Communist Party, would install public ownership of basic industries and state planning of economic goals. Workers in each factory would have a decisive voice in running their plant. The party soft-pedals talk of such extreme measures as abolition of private property and collectivization.

But the angry young militants of the New Left see little chance of a peaceful transition from capitalism to socialism. They talk of revolution and guerrilla warfare. To them the symbol of authority is the policeman, whom they call "pig." To these young radicals, police are fair targets for rocks and bottles and other weapons. So, too, are campus buildings and Selective Service offices. So far their violence has been directed primarily at property. But guns are becoming more common. At Cornell University, black students reinforced their demands for change by taking over a building and arming themselves with rifles.

Extremist groups, such as the Black Panthers, teach their members how to make and use Molotov cocktails. The Panthers also are setting up schools in California to teach guerrilla warfare

Who's Who on the Far Left

Communist Party-U.S.A. (CP-USA)

Position: U.S. branch of the international Communist Party. Policy comes directly from Moscow.

Leadership: Gus Hall, general secretary: Henry W. Winston; Claude Lightfoot; Michael Zagarell; Daniel Rubin; Herbert Aptheker.

Location: Headquarters, New York City; membership estimated at between 12,000 and 13,000.

Character: Predominantly white adults.

Brief History: Founded in Chicago, Illinois, September 1, 1919. Poverty and the U.S. depression helped strengthen party during the 1930s. It polled 100,000 votes for its presidential candidate in 1932. Hitler-Stalin Pact of World War II, preceding the German invasion of Russia, caused many U.S. members to drop out of the party. After the war, CP-USA went underground to escape the 1940 Smith Act, which made it a crime to conspire, advocate, or teach the violent overthrow of the government; and the 1950 McCarran Act, which required registration of members. By mid-'50s, Senator Joseph McCarthy had died; the Smith Act was "gutted"; the McCarran Act registration requirement was ruled unconstitutional. The party returned to its open activities.

Although the Moscow brand of communism is considered reactionary by much of the New Left, party membership has increased about 25% since 1960. In 1968, the party had an official presidential candidate on the national ballot for the first time in 28 years. July 1968, Zagarell reported that "the student unrest on the college campuses and the anti-draft demonstrations have been helped along by the Communist Party." The party's youth group, the W. E. B. DuBois Clubs, had less than 100 members in March 1969, but party officials claim much of their own new membership consists of young people. At the May 1969 national convention, Hall cautioned that "it is not yet time to organize armed struggle;" but the party's Commission on Black Liberation approves "cooperation" with BPP.

techniques.

"Our primary task is to build a Marxist-Leninist revolutionary movement," says Michael Klonsky, former national secretary of Students for a Democratic Society (SDS), largest of the New Left groups. In a television interview, Klonsky described the American system as "racist," "capitalist," and "imperialist," and urged student radicals to arm themselves. "I believe we are going to have revolutionary change in the society," he said.

The New Leftists offer no clear view of what their future society would be like. They talk of socialism, communism, and Marxism. But their real emphasis is on tearing down rather than on building up. They are interested in a transfer of power from

Allen Young, center, of the SDS press service, meets with newsmen at the 1969 SDS convention in Chicago. He is flanked by Bernardine Dohrn and Michael Klonsky, self-described "revolutionary communists" who held national offices during the 1968-69 school year.

Who's Who on the Far Left
Students for a Democratic Society (SDS)

Position: Leadership advocates overthrow of the U.S. "system."

Leadership: Mark Rudd, Milton Rosen, Jeffrey Gordon, Michael Klonsky, Carl Davidson, Rennie Davis, Alan Haber, Tom Hayden, Bernardine Dohrn, Carl Oglesby.

Location: Headquarters, Chicago; an estimated 500 branches.

Character: Membership of 30,000 to 70,000, predominantly white, middle-class students. Within SDS, feuding independent groups are competing for power. Major factions include Rudd's Revolutionary Youth Movement I, the 1969 elected leadership; Klonsky's Revolutionary Youth Movement II; and Rosen's Progressive Labor Party. RYM I rejects the guidance of Moscow and Peking, but embraces Marxist-Leninist theory.

Brief History: In 1959, Student League for Industrial Democracy, offspring of League for Industrial Democracy, changed its name to SDS under Haber. June 1962, Hayden's Port Huron Statement advocating reform (not revolution) for the United States was adopted. 1964, SDS had 1,200 members in 27 chapters. Radical Education Project was established at Ann Arbor, Michigan, to circulate SDS literature, speakers, and films. February 1965, U.S. bombing of North Vietnam began. Spring 1965, SDS had 125 chapters with 4,000 members. June 1965, SDS dropped clause in constitution barring "advocates and apologists of totalitarianism." LID severed all ties with SDS. June 1968, revolutionary communists were elected national leaders. From October 1967 to May 1969, 211 campuses were involved in 471 disruptions, causing millions of dollars in damage.

Since December 1963, when SDS voted to accept "local insurgency" as the organization's purpose, guerrilla warfare and arson techniques have been featured in SDS literature. January 1969, Cameron Bishop became the first SDSer to make the FBI's Ten Most Wanted Men List on suspicion of sabotage. As one SDSer emphasized in June 1969: "It's not reform we're after."

one group to another, without explaining what the successor might be.

For example, when Clark Kissinger, a former SDS national secretary, was asked about socialism, he replied: "We don't take positions on that sort of thing. What we don't like about the liberal welfare state is that all decisions are made in Washington. . . . We don't want to tell the poor what the solutions to their problems should be. Once American democracy is revitalized, we'll let the poor decide for themselves what solutions they want."

There is a strong streak of anarchism running through New Left ideology. Many of its members express violent opposition to all government authority. They come close to advocating the abolition of government rather than seeking the increased government control that would come with socialism.

The anticapitalist philosophy of Karl Marx is a common thread running through all groups on the far left. Social inequality and injustice are considered to be inevitable results of the capitalist system. They follow Marx's view that private ownership of industry brings exploitation and degradation of the working class.

If overthrow of the capitalist system is the long-range goal of the far left, how do they propose to achieve it? What are their immediate goals?

Leaders of the orthodox Communist Party have no illusions about the chances of overturning the capitalist system in the United States. They recognize that a "revolutionary situation" does not exist at present, notwithstanding all the noise and violence on campuses and in the cities. This might be expected to develop over a long period of time, and as a result of intensive proselytizing work by the Communist Party. The present aim is to persist year after year in spreading communist doctrines until they have undermined confidence in the established order and have produced a minority sufficiently large and powerful to overwhelm it.

Immediate goals of the Communist Party are:

• To gain respectability. An intensive effort is under way to remake the party's image and secure its acceptance as a legitimate political party.

Gus Hall, center, Communist Party secretary general, raises hands of Mrs. Charlene Mitchell and Michael Zagarell after they were nominated as the party's candidates respectively for the offices of president and vice president of the United States in 1968. This was the first time since 1940 that the Communist Party ran a presidential ticket.

• To gain control of the New Left. Party leaders recognize that winning control of these young people who already consider themselves Marxists is the key to the party's future.

• To expand its influence within the labor and civil rights movements.

• To sustain attacks on American foreign policy, particularly wherever it is in conflict with communist movements throughout the world. The principal tactic is to picture the U.S. government as the ally of corrupt, right-wing dictatorships. Another is to try to spread public discontent with Vietnam policy to all foreign policy moves.

The drive for respectability began when the party won its long court battle against laws requiring it to register as a communist action group and agent of the Soviet Union. A series of Supreme Court rulings between 1962 and 1965 upheld the party contention that registration would violate constitutional protection against self-incrimination.

The court victories freed the party to operate in the open. In June 1966 it held its first national convention in two decades. Two years later, with press and television coverage, the party nominated a presidential ticket. Mrs. Charlene Mitchell, a 38-year-old Negro from California, was its candidate for president, and Michael Zagarell, a 23-year-old party youth leader from New York, was the vice presidential candidate.

The Communists followed many of the traditions of American political conventions. There were nominating speeches, and after the ticket was chosen by acclamation the candidates stood in the traditional pose, their hands held high above their heads, to acknowledge the cheers of the delegates. Like Democrats and Republicans, the Communists adopted a party platform. Its planks included a demand to pull out of Vietnam immediately and to "begin dismantling the military-industrial complex." There also were calls to "change the tax structure to soak the rich" and to "end police brutality."

The party had no hope of victory or even of being a significant factor. Its ticket was on the ballot only in Minnesota and Washington and received 1,075 votes out of a total of 73 million cast.

W. E. B. DuBois, founder of the clubs bearing his name, which are the youth group of the Communist Party-U.S.A.

The W.E.B. DuBois Clubs of America are among the many organizations seeking membership or support on the college campuses.

But Communist leaders were interested not so much in votes as in a platform from which to preach and to convert the public. The party is tiny. Its membership is estimated to be about 14,000, with perhaps 100,000 sympathizers.

Seeking every chance to speak and be heard, party leaders developed their college speaking program. The party sent letters to campus groups volunteering to supply speakers. On campuses it delivered its view to its prime target—young people.

Youth groups have long been fixtures in party operations. They often were set up as party fronts. One of the most recent such cases, according to the Justice Department, involved the DuBois Clubs of America. When the government sought to force the clubs to register as a communist front group in 1966, it described the group as dominated from its inception by the Communist Party-U.S.A.

For several years, during the period of frequent mass antiwar demonstrations, the DuBois Clubs prospered. Their members were regarded as among the most skilled organizers on the left. They were masters of the techniques of recruiting well-known people from outside the extreme left to serve on organizations for antiwar demonstrations. Bettina Aptheker, daughter of Communist Party theoretician Herbert Aptheker, an admitted communist herself, was one of the most active members.

However, the clubs were regarded by many of the long-haired New Leftists as "square." As the number of mass antiwar demonstrations declined, so did the DuBois Clubs. According to the FBI, club membership dropped to less than 100. In March 1969, the Communist Party held a West Coast Youth Conference at which, the FBI reports, "it was deemed necessary to change the concept of the organization from a massive-type organization to a young Communist organization."

The decline of the DuBois Clubs led the Communist Party to turn its attention to SDS. Here was the most active leftist youth group in the country. Its members already had proclaimed their belief in Marxism.

But the Communist Party faces competition in its bid to gain control of SDS. The pro-Peking Progressive Labor Party and

Who's Who on the Far Left
Young Socialist Alliance (YSA)

Position: Supports Marxist-Leninist theories as interpreted by Leon Trotsky; advocates worldwide revolution to establish international communism. Pro-Castro, anti-Moscow, anti-Peking.

Leadership: Larry Seigle, national chairman; Carol Lipman; Nelson Blackstock.

Location: Headquarters, New York City; groups sponsored at high schools and colleges across the country.

Character: Predominantly white, radical student group; the largest Trotskyite faction in the SDS. It is the youth group of the Socialist Workers Party (SWP), the U.S. branch of an international revolutionary movement.

Brief History: Four young Trotskyite groups are vying for influence within SDS: Youth Against War and Fascism, of the Workers World Party; the Sparticist League; the Johnson-Forrest group; and YSA. YSA is currently the strongest of these, claiming membership in 101 colleges and universities, 32 high schools, and 5 junior high schools.

They control the Student Mobilization Committee to End the War in Vietnam (SMC), which is the youth group of the National Mobilization Committee to End the War in Vietnam (NMC). The parent organization is a loose coalition of radical groups which, according to Senate testimony, provided major leadership at the Chicago Convention rioting, as well as for the assault on the Pentagon in 1967.

The eighth national convention of YSA in December 1968 at Chicago attracted 800 and featured Black Panther Party speakers. The group fully supports armed black guerrilla warfare.

other Marxist groups are challenging it. The contest between rival Marxist groups flared into the open at the SDS national convention in June 1969. By the time the convention ended, the organization had split in two, with each faction meeting separately and claiming to represent the majority.

The potential value of the New Left to the communists can be seen in the influence these young people are trying to exert in areas where the Communist Party has been stymied for years. For example, in the labor movement, it is the New Left, not the Old, that hopes to influence union members. In the immediate postwar years, the labor movement methodically purged communists from its ranks. Communist dominated unions were expelled. Some labor leaders who had flirted with communism turned from it and, in many cases, became militant anticommunists. It was the end of party influence in organized labor.

The way seemed to be open to the New Left. Its members talk about forming a student-worker alliance. They take summer jobs in factories in order to spread their ideas. And many strikers are surprised to find young New Leftists, uninvited, joining their picket lines to show their sympathy with the union cause.

As New Left influence grows among labor and civil rights groups, communists expect their own influence to expand along with it. While communists do not control SDS and similar groups, they are, in the words of Gus Hall, organizations which the party has "going for us."

The party's greatest gains have been in the antiwar movement. Here was a cause which appealed to many Americans. At first, the antiwar movement was made up mostly of traditional pacifists and members of the far left. But as the war dragged on, opposition to it grew. Members of Congress began speaking out against the American effort. Massive antiwar demonstrations were held, many of them with the help of skilled communist organizers, attracting large numbers of people who were not communists or even leftists.

The communists found themselves associated with a cause that had mass support. Here was another opportunity for public exposure and for persuading people to accept communists as

Who's Who on the Far Left
Progressive Labor Party (PLP)

Position: Dedicated to revolutionary Marxism as advocated by Mao Tse-tung. Imports political material from Cuba and Peking. Advocates "Worker-Student Alliance" as essential for revolution. In the words of Jeffrey Gordon, "We are not pacifists," but desire to build "a world of revolutionary socialism."

Leadership: Milton Rosen, chairman; Jeffrey Gordon; John Pennington; Jared Israel; William Epton; Allen Krebs.

Location: Headquarters, New York City. Membership is found primarily on college campuses within the SDS, which it seeks to control. Current stronghold: New England.

Character: Membership predominantly white, middle-class, radical students. The group is highly disciplined and frowns on drugs, long hair.

Brief History: Founded by Mortimer Scher and Milton Rosen in 1962 following their expulsion from the Communist Party-U.S.A. because of Maoist sentiments. Originally the Progressive Labor Movement, it assumed present name around 1965.

Front organizations include May Second Movement (M2M), Student Committee for Travel to Cuba, Harlem Defense Council, Committee to Defend Resistance to Ghetto Life, and Free University of New York (now the Free School: curriculum includes such courses as "Marxism and American Decadence"). M2M was founded at Yale University on March 14, 1964. In 1966 it was dissolved and the membership of about 1,000 was instructed, according to Senate testimony, to infiltrate such groups as SDS and SNCC to radicalize membership.

In 1967, the Communist Party of Red China informed top-level members that it considered PLP the only revolutionary Marxist-Leninist party in the United States. At the June 1969 convention of SDS, this group demonstrated its strength by nearly gaining control of the organization.

Americans comparable to those belonging to other minority parties. James Davis, writing in *Political Affairs*, a journal published by the party, said, "It is in the peace movement where party spokesmen gain the ear of people who never heard, much less spoke to a communist."

The effect of the Vietnam war on young people is expected to bring long-range benefits to the extreme left. Radical leaders on campuses say that without the war their organizations probably would not exist. Nearly every issue for which New Leftists have been able to win mass support among students is directly related to the war. They include ROTC programs, on-campus recruitment by the military and by defense industries, and research work done by universities for the Pentagon.

Thus the Vietnam war has been a major factor in the formation of the New Left, and it developed into an issue which neither the New Left nor the communists could easily afford to lose. The irony is that the declared primary goal of both is to bring the Vietnam war to an end.

Some leaders of the New Left, fearing that the end of the war could also bring an end to their movement, are looking ahead to the postwar period and searching for other grounds on which to base a continuation of their work.

For example, David Pugh, a member of the SDS at Stanford University, says:

> There may be some dogmatic types who disagree, but I don't think the Vietnam war is a visible issue as such any more. ... Even the trustees want to get out of the war now. It's not good business any more. So we have to make an issue out of war itself. . . . We are trying to get liberals to understand that Vietnam was no aberration, that there is a war machine built into our system.

Other objectives in the SDS armory which could assume increasing importance in the future are the following:

• To change the structure of universities to secure for students a greater voice at all levels of administration.

Who's Who on the Far Left
Youth International Party (Yippies)

Position: Avowed aim is to destroy "The Man"—their term for the Establishment and its present system of government. Their message to young people: Revolution is fun.

Leadership: Jerry Rubin, Paul Krassner, Ed Sanders, Abbie Hoffman, Keith Lampe.

Location: Active in New York City, Chicago, and Berkeley. No formal organization.

Character: Small group of white radicals whose dress and speech is purposefully outrageous in an effort to appeal to young people as the antithesis of "stuffiness."

Brief History: Conceived of in 1967 by Abbie Hoffman to attract hippies into revolutionary activity. The group was officially founded on January 1, 1968, by several young men, including past members of PLP, SNCC, and SDS.

They are especially attracted to "guerrilla theater" techniques designed to make officials and police appear ridiculous or vicious to young people. As Jerry Rubin (PLP) put it in the November 16, 1967, issue of the Village Voice: "See you next August in Chicago at the Democratic National Convention. Bring pot, fake delegates' cards, smoke bombs, costumes, blood to throw, and all kinds of interesting props."

The Yippie gospel is spread through a network of some 200 newspapers—the Underground Press—in items such as this one in a Washington Free Press: "Even if Chicago does not burn, the paranoia and guilt of the government will force them to bring in thousands of troops, and the more troops, the better the theater."

As one member sees their contribution: "Yippies are chipping away, blacks are chipping away, the enemy overseas is chipping away. If you keep on hitting the Man from every side, punching him, laughing at him, ridiculing him, he will eventually collapse. That's what is going to happen in America."

- To change the structure of society to secure "more power" for the "people."
- To sustain challenges to established authority, described in New Left circles as the "politics of confrontation."
- To awaken the masses to what New Left theorists call the "evils" of the capitalist system.

Next to Vietnam, the New Left found that the issue with greatest appeal was the way universities are run. As American universities have grown, they have become more impersonal. Students found themselves in lecture halls seating several hundred. Many professors, involved in research projects, were seen by students only during lectures. It was common for students to refer to such universities as "factories."

The first attack on the structure of universities occurred in 1964 at the University of California at Berkeley. A dispute over whether a section of university property could be used for political rallies was the issue that quickly escalated into the so-called Free Speech Movement. Mass demonstrations kept the university paralyzed for days.

Many extreme leftists, including Miss Aptheker, were prominently involved in the Berkeley demonstrations.

Berkeley showed how such a demonstration could swiftly paralyze a university. It became a model for similar demonstrations which spread over campuses throughout the nation.

At first, students demanded more freedom, particularly within living quarters, and a larger say in governing the universities. Then the protests spread to attacks on the relationship between universities and the government, many of these being related to the war. These evolved into ideological attacks. Miss Aptheker, for example, denounced universities as tools of "those who control the system of state monopoly capitalism." She pictured the universities as being used by industry as a training ground for technicians, as research centers, and as a means for indoctrinating young people. She described universities as "ideological centers for the defense of this system."

The more militant New Leftists reject reforms that give students greater power. They contend that "the influence of the

A. J. Muste (second from right) presides at a rally in 1966 honoring recent Hanoi visitors Herbert Aptheker, CP-USA (left); Tom Hayden of SDS; and (far right) Staughton Lynd, whose politics are "pro-Moscow." Their trip violated State Department restrictions.

Bettina Aptheker, member of the Communist Party-U.S.A.'s national committee, addresses a noontime rally of 2,000 students at the University of California at Berkeley, urging them to form a power block with the faculty in order to "have the say" in the selection of the new university president.

university must be destroyed. We cannot do that by opportun-istically building the student power illusion that we can reform the university into serving the people under capitalism."

Some members of the New Left, looking ahead, want to shift the movement away from its university base and spread it out among the general population. Tom Hayden, a founder of SDS, started community action projects in 10 cities. His aim was to have young people live among the poor, help them organize themselves, and show them how to gain some power.

The most successful of his projects was carried out in Newark, New Jersey. Hayden, himself, led this project. Protests organized by SDS helped the city's poor obtain better garbage collection and tenement repairs. However, the accomplishments of the project were largely wiped out by the six days of bloody rioting that erupted in Newark in July 1967.

The New Left is a loose grouping of many organizations. The largest is SDS, with a membership variously estimated at from 40,000 to 70,000 followers on 500 campuses. SDS keeps no mem-bership figures. Dues of $2 are not mandatory for membership. A chapter's strength and size lie in the issues it raises and the support it can muster. SDS maintains a national headquarters in Chicago and elects a national secretary each year at a convention. But the national office has no control over individual chapters.

Free love and marijuana are part of the SDS image, but mem-bers of a minority of the SDS which seeks to take over the majority, the Progressive Labor Party, shun marijuana and com-munal living. They tend to dress neatly and to wear short hair. They are highly disciplined and militant. Because of their adher-ence to the doctrines of Mao Tse-tung, the Progressive Laborites often are referred to by their rivals as the "Mao Now crowd."

In an effort to keep the organization from breaking up, many SDS chapters elect multiple leaderships reflecting different fac-tions. The Harvard University chapter had three co-chairmen, each representing a different faction.

Whereas SDS is almost entirely white, another wing of the New Left is exclusively black. The principal black organizations are the Student Nonviolent Coordinating Committee (SNCC), which sprang from the old civil rights movement, and the Black Panthers, which began as a black nationalist group preaching violence and then added the philosophy of Marxism. Indicating a trend, the Student Nonviolent Coordinating Committee recently dropped "Nonviolent" from its name and substituted the word "National."

SNCC once had many white members, but since the advent of Black Power, it has become almost entirely black. The Panthers have no white members, but the group, on some occasions, has cooperated with SDS. When Eldridge Cleaver, the best-known and most articulate of the Panther leaders, began advocating alliances with poor whites, he split on this issue with Stokely Carmichael, another leader. Carmichael resigned from the Panthers and warned the party against trying to form alliances with whites. Cleaver replied, "It has always seemed to me that you belittle the intelligence of your black brothers and sisters when you constantly warn them that they had better beware of white folks."

At the same time, Cleaver defended the steady move leftward by the Panthers. "If you look around the world," he wrote, "you will see that the only countries which have liberated themselves and managed to withstand the tide of counter-revolution are precisely those countries that have strongly Marxist-Leninist parties."

The loose organization and constant squabbling within the ranks of the New Left stand in sharp contrast with the tight organization and discipline of the Communist Party.

Party policy is carried out by the National Executive Committee headed by Hall as general secretary. Regional chairmen and secretaries are responsible for such areas as education and labor. The committee is the equivalent of the central committee of the Soviet Communist Party.

As in the case of the Soviet constitution, party rules call for democracy at all levels. All issues are to be decided by majority vote. But, as in the Soviet government, there is little democracy in actual practice. Discipline is the byword, and those who refuse to accept it face expulsion. Policy is set at the top, and loyal functionaries see to it that lower levels agree.

Insistence on following the party line has led to periodic up-

Stokely Carmichael, an early and eloquent advocate of Black Power "by any means necessary" rose through the ranks of SNCC to become the prime minister of the Black Panther Party in 1968. An inveterate world traveler, the Trinidad-born revolutionary is now living in Africa.

Eldridge Cleaver, exiled minister of information of the BPP and international editor of Ramparts magazine, is seen during balmier days speaking to a campus crowd as the presidential candidate of the Peace and Freedom Party.

heavals within the party. The latest occurred after the Soviet invasion of Czechoslovakia. Party leaders in New York and California resigned after a hastily called party convention voted by a narrow margin to censure all members who refused to sanction the Soviet move.

While policy is carried out by the committee, it is largely set by Moscow. This does not mean that someone sitting in the Soviet Union is always directing the American party to follow this or that policy. But the Communist Party-U.S.A. is regarded by observers as the most loyal to Moscow of the world's Communist parties. While many European Communist parties were critical of the Soviet invasion of Czechoslovakia, Gus Hall and Herbert Aptheker were quick to defend the move.

The Communist Party is often short of money. Publication of the *Daily Worker* was reduced to once a week for a time because of lack of funds. However, in 1966 Harry Herman Kaplan, a wealthy Brooklyn, New York, builder, died and left half his $2.6 million estate to the party. With that money party officials were able to start up another newspaper, the *Daily World,* and issue it five days a week. The party has received other, smaller bequests from time to time.

Some American experts believe foreign communist governments have given financial help to U.S. communists. Richard H. Sanger, author of *Insurgent Era* and an expert on guerrilla warfare, points out, in an interview with *U.S.News & World Report,* that organizers of the antiwar March on the Pentagon in 1967 were able to supply 100 buses plus other equipment, lodging, and meals. Where did the money come from? According to Sanger, "The money becomes available when the party leaders need it."

"Legitimate pacifist organizations paid for much of the October show [at the Pentagon]. But a lot of cash or gold for such a peace demonstration comes from Russia, from China or from North Vietnam, which is most directly concerned."

For normal, day-to-day operations, the Communist Party and the New Left depend largely on contributions. In testimony before the House Appropriations Committee, FBI director J. Edgar Hoover said most contributions are in the $10 to $50 range.

Wealthy supporters, he said, have contributed more than $100,000 to the New Left. New Leftists also often take up collections at antiwar demonstrations. Hoover stated that $25,000 was collected during the 1967 March on the Pentagon.

Another source of funds is Resist, an organization based in Cambridge, Massachusetts, which aids draft resisters. Formed in 1967 by a group of professors, writers, and ministers, Resist gives thousands of dollars each year to aid antidraft organizations.

Heavily armed members of Cornell University's Afro-American Society are seen leaving the student center they occupied to force a change in university policies, April 1969. The group now refers to itself as the Black Liberation Front (BLF).

However, even large gifts such as Kaplan's leave both the New and Old Left in tight financial straits. And life on the extreme left in the United States can be very difficult. Those who choose it often are motivated by convictions.

Gus Hall, for example, was one of 11 communist leaders jailed in 1949 under the Smith Act, later declared unconstitutional. He served his sentence in a maximum security cell in Leavenworth next to the late "Machinegun" Kelly, the bank robber of the 1930s. Henry Winston, party national chairman, went blind while serving his Smith Act sentence.

In the 1950s, at the height of congressional investigations of communist penetration of government, any communist association could lead to a person being barred from public employment. The party was forced to remain underground during that period—a political party unable to put forth candidates or mount a campaign.

Those grim days are over. Hall, a native of Minnesota and a former steelworker, is the picture of affability. His message is moderation, socialism "Made in U.S.A."

He was not always that way. In 1934, Hall was asked in a court trial:

"Are you willing to fight and overthrow this government?"

"Absolutely," he replied.

"And you are willing to take up arms and overthrow the constituted authorities?"

"When the time comes, yes."

Hall's counterpart in the pro-Peking Progressive Labor Party is Milton Rosen. To Rosen there is no chance of a peaceful transition to socialism. He told an audience at the University of North Carolina: "The ultimate revolutionary demand is a government controlled by the working people . . . a revolutionary dictatorship of armed workers."

Among the smaller, less noticed factions on the Old Left is the Socialist Workers Party. This group follows the teachings of Leon Trotsky, one of the leaders of the Russian Revolution. Trotsky was a militant advocate of trying to export the Soviet revolution to other nations. But he lost out in a power struggle with Stalin after the death of Lenin. Trotsky went into exile in Mexico, where he was assassinated by a man reputed to have been an agent of Stalin.

Lew Jones, a graduate of Northwestern University and a member of a middle-class southern family, is a Trotskyite. "By instinct, I was a rebel," he says. "I am a socialist because I believe it to be the only system that can solve the problems of the world. I am a Trotskyite because I believe he, Trotsky, is the only one to correctly interpret Marx."

It was the depression that drove many of the older members of the far left to turn to Marx. The depression seemed to confirm Marx's theories about business cycles becoming more and more extreme and eventually leading to the collapse of capitalism.

But the nation's economic system did not collapse. Instead, it became stronger. Why, then, during a period of unprecedented prosperity, have so many young people turned against the established order and toward the left?

The answer is not a simple one, and those who have studied the problem advance a number of reasons. Among other things, they say, young people are outraged by some of the aspects of present-day life which accompany our prosperity. These include:

• An increasingly automated, computerized society in which the machine appears to be taking over and man is being reduced to a number. This tends to make life more and more impersonal, unfriendly, and "unnatural."

• Persistent poverty and slums which cast an ugly light on the general image of affluence in the United States.

• Pollution, congestion, and similar unpleasant consequences of population explosion and disorderly urban growth.

• Persistent racial discrimination and seemingly slow progress in correcting it.

• A growing bureaucracy which seems to be running away with the government, over which the individual feels he has lost control.

• Increasing complexity of military and foreign affairs in a pushbutton age of missiles. These seem to place such matters as war and peace also beyond control of the individual, adding to

SDS national headquarters in Chicago, Illinois. From here the organization's annually elected officials seek to coordinate the activities of 26 regional offices and 500 branch offices.

his frustration.

Thus, according to students of the problem, many young people turn against the established order because the affluence it produces is accompanied by too many aspects which are unacceptable to them, including a seemingly endless war in Vietnam. Among those rejecting these negative aspects of contemporary life are some well educated, intelligent young men and women coming from extremely wealthy families.

What can young people, especially those with a sense of idealism, do about such matters as pollution, overpopulation, crime, corruption, racial discrimination, war?

The simplest thing is to plunge into an emotional outburst, take an irrational approach, and damn the established order together with all the ills surrounding it. That is just about what the 65 students from 11 colleges did in 1962 when they met at Port Huron, Michigan, and founded SDS.

The emotional feeling of outrage explains many of the wild, irrational acts committed by the young people of the New Left, both on and off the campus. The lack of a rational approach helps explain why they have not been able to produce any clear plan of what order they would install in place of the one they seek to destroy.

Sociologist Daniel Bell says: "At best, the New Left is all heart. At worst, it is no mind."

This is an ideal situation for communists and for the countries behind them, notably Soviet Russia and Communist China. Communism, as practiced today, makes its strongest appeal outside communist countries to those whose emotions cloud their reason.

It may be true, as one commentator remarked, that many New Leftists who describe themselves as socialists cannot tell socialism from rheumatism. But communists can recognize an opportunity when they see one. And in the New Left, with its "new coat" of many colors, communists of all varieties have found a chance to get back into business in the United States in a big way.

Leaders of the New Left may have no clear idea of what would replace the established order they seek to depose, but professional communists do. And these communists are prepared to supply the answers which the New Left apparently lacks. What they expect of the New Left are persistent attacks which will demoralize new generations of American citizens and eventually undermine the pillars of the established, capitalist order. In time, they believe this will come to pass. The professional communists would then undertake to look after the rest.

Chapter Two

How They Exploit War

For communist countries, notably Soviet Russia and Communist China, there are two kinds of war, described as "just" and "unjust."

A "just" war, in fact, as distinguished in Marxist jargon, is any war which advances the territorial, political, economic, or any other interest of a communist country. An "unjust" war is one which does not serve such an interest.

(A war between two communist countries, such as Russia and China, represents something of a nightmare for Marxist theoreticians in applying their definition of just and unjust wars.)

In the case of communist parties outside communist countries, wars have still another dimension. They are supported or opposed by these parties, depending on which side communist countries happen to be involved with. At the same time, they provide an occasion for the party either to prosper or to shrivel, depending on the amount of national support for the war effort and the side on which the party finds itself.

For example, at the outset of World War II, Stalin joined Hitler in dismembering Poland. The American people, strongly sympathizing with the victim, felt outraged. When the Communist Party in the United States sought to defend the Hitler-Stalin act of aggression, it fell into such disgrace that it still has not recovered and perhaps never will completely recover from this particular experience so long as there are Americans who remember it.

On the other hand, the Vietnam war is a very different story. In this case, as the conflict dragged on, seemingly without end, the ground became ripe for opposition. Here was an opportunity for the communists to fertilize the ground and to reap benefits both for themselves and for the communist countries abroad with which they are associated.

Opposition to the war in the United States served to strengthen the bargaining position of the communist countries. It also led to a kind of "popular front" movement in which communists could mingle freely as an ally in a common cause.

Bettina Aptheker, daughter of Communist Party-U.S.A. leader Herbert Aptheker, has been active in the antiwar movement.

For a tiny group such as the communists in the United States, the "popular front" tactic is the only one through which it can multiply its influence out of all proportion to its numbers and have a serious impact on the course of American policy. Vietnam made such a tactic possible. In association with the New Left, the communists exploited it to the full.

Vietnam Week demonstrations in the spring of 1967 provide a good example of how they operated.

The idea for Vietnam Week can be traced to an article in the spring 1966 issue of *Dimensions,* the publication of the DuBois Clubs of America. It was written by Bettina Aptheker. She suggested "a nationwide student-faculty strike in September when hundreds of thousands walk out for several hours one fine day and say get out of Vietnam."

Having been a leader of the 1964 demonstrations at the University of California at Berkeley, Miss Aptheker had become one of the best-known communists in America.

In calling for a nationwide antiwar demonstration, Miss Aptheker said, "There are two major things required in the peace movement today: bringing ever larger numbers of people into the movement, with the greatest degree of unity possible, and avoidance at all costs of the isolation of the Left. Second, we must increase the militancy of the movement."

In speaking engagements over the next several weeks, usually on campuses, Miss Aptheker frequently repeated her call for mass protest. However, the September target date could not be met, and it was decided to hold the demonstrations the week of April 8-15, 1967.

A great deal of organizational work is involved in such a large demonstration. A Student Strike for Peace Committee was formed. Sponsors included Miss Aptheker, Franklin Alexander, chairman of the DuBois Clubs, and Anthony Wilkinson and Frank Emspak, both sons of Communist Party members. There were 33 sponsors in all at this stage.

Then letters were sent out to prospective additional sponsors. Signed by Jean Loftus of the temporary organizing committee, Student Strike for Peace, the letters noted: "At present the strike is identified in many people's minds only with Bettina Aptheker, whose proposal it initially was. Since late this summer, when Bettina originally proposed this strike, many people representing an impressive cross-section of the academic community have endorsed the call for a December planning meeting."

By the time that meeting was held at the University of Chicago at the end of December, the number of sponsors had grown to 193. Sponsors included 12 members of the Communist Party and five members of the Trotskyite youth group, the Young Socialist Alliance. Another 14 members of the Young Socialist Alliance attended the conference as did 3 members of its parent group, the Socialist Workers Party. Three members of the Progressive Labor Party also were on hand.

One of the Progressive Labor delegates expressed that militant group's distaste for the conference in a article in *Challenge*, the party's official publication. "The conference was dominated," he wrote, "by the Communist Party of the United States, the DuBois Clubs and the Young Socialist Alliance. It refused to consider 'politics for advancing the movement,' suggested by Students for a Democratic Society and the Progressive Labor Party."

The rhetoric of the conference was familiar. The Vietnam war was described in the conference's "Call to Vietnam Week" as "a racist war, a murderous war against a colored people . . . an illegal war." The issues of the Vietnam Week demonstrations would be "(1) bringing the GIs home now; (2) opposing the draft, and supporting the right of individuals to refuse to cooperate with the military system; and (3) ending campus complicity with the war effort."

Communists played a major role at the Chicago conference, but they were not alone. Among the other groups represented were the American Friends Service Committee, the National Student Association, SNCC, Congress of Racial Equality, and the Southern Christian Leadership Conference.

The same had been true a month earlier at Cleveland, Ohio, when another group that was to play a major role in the Vietnam Week demonstrations had been formed. It was the Spring Mobilization Committee.

An enraged University of Wisconsin student yells at police, protesting their use of riot clubs and tear gas to break up an antiwar protest demonstration against the Dow Chemical Company. Dozens of persons, including police, were injured in the rioting at Madison, Wisconsin.

President of the committee was A. J. Muste of the Fellowship of Reconciliation, a leading American pacifist. One of the vice chairmen was another pacifist, David Dellinger.

No communists were listed among the officers. But many were active in the committee, including Bettina Aptheker; Albert Lima, chairman of the Northern California District of the Communist Party; Ben Dobbs, a leader of the party's Southern California District; Arnold Johnson, public relations director of the Communist Party; and James R. Lindsay, who was a Communist Party candidate for city councilman in San Jose, California.

The committee started a magazine, *Mobilizer,* and in the first issue, Muste discussed the problem of trying to broaden the

Burning draft cards became a successful device for mobilizing students in an antiwar movement. The New Left thrived on demonstrations of this kind.

movement's base to attract the "ordinary run of American citizens." Some members of the movement, he noted, think of these ordinary American citizens as "well-meaning but deceived and ill-informed about what is going on in Vietnam. They conclude that these people must be approached with a 'moderate' program."

Muste supported a nonexclusion policy—allowing any group, including communists, to play a part in the movement. "We adhere to the policy of non-exclusion, first and most of all, because it is right in principle.... People of the Left (Communists with or without quotation marks) should be permitted and expected to function normally in the political life of the country."

Muste added, "In practice, a non-communist coalition is in danger of becoming an anti-communist one.... What no doubt clinches the matter is that if we were to abandon the non-exclusion principle we would quickly disintegrate."

Muste spoke for the faction that believed all groups opposed to the Vietnam war should be admitted into the antiwar movement. Another faction felt that the presence of known communists would dilute the movement's effectiveness. They believed that the American people would never buy the arguments of any group in which it could be demonstrated that communists played a significant role.

The communists themselves seemed to accept at least the conclusion of the second group. By the time the Vietnam Week demonstrations were held, most communists, so active in the early organizational phase, had faded into the background.

The final day of Vietnam Week rallies were held in New York and San Francisco. There wasn't a communist in sight at either rally. The main speaker at the New York rally was Martin Luther King. His wife addressed the San Francisco rally. An estimated 180,000 people attended the two protest meetings.

The question of communist participation was raised two days later when Secretary of State Dean Rusk and Dr. King appeared on separate television interview programs.

"I have no doubt at all," Rusk said, "that the communist apparatus is very busy indeed in these operations all over the world and in our own country. But I don't mean to say by that that all those who have objections to the war in Vietnam are communists. But the worldwide communist movement is working very hard on this."

Dr. King's position was: "I don't think the communists played any significant part. . . . The people protesting the war are by and large patriotic Americans."

Certainly, as we have seen, the communists were active in organizing the Vietnam Week protests. But the 180,000 people who attended the rallies were, for the most part, patriotic Americans concerned about what they felt was a mistaken venture costing many lives.

Investigations of the House Committee on Un-American Activities checked the background of the Vietnam Week protest and reached this conclusion: "The proposal for a nationwide student strike was completely communist in origin."

To the extent that the idea did originate with Bettina Aptheker and that much of the early organizational work was done by communists, the committee could not be disputed.

Another mass antiwar demonstration, a March on the Pentagon, was held in October 1967. The day before it started, a Pentagon spokesman told newsmen that there were individuals in the administration committee of the sponsoring organization "who by their statements and by press reports have been identified as communists or communist sympathizers." However, he said the communists did not represent a large number and were not in control of the protest.

Sanger gave this description of their activities at the Pentagon demonstration:

Of about 50,000 marchers, I would say 40,000 were pacifists and other people who don't approve of war in general and this one in particular. Then there were about 9,500 "hippies," "flower children," "beatniks," etc.—some of the strangest characters you can imagine. And then a small corps—probably 200 in all—were the activists whom you could spot when they moved in. At times they surrounded their speakers to protect them. At other times they formed cordons or linked arms to clear the way. It was they who were giving the directions, and it was no accident that some $10,000 worth of loudspeaker equipment was there for them to use. . . .

I'm sure the communists and active pacifists were watching for recruits at the Pentagon. Of the 50,000 persons of all types who turned up, if they found five new people who fitted in to their disciplined, dedicated pattern, the exercise was worth it from their point of view.

David Dellinger was one of the leaders of the Pentagon protest. Asked by newsmen if he were a communist, Dellinger replied:

David Dellinger, chairman of the National Mobilization Committee to End the War in Vietnam, discusses plans for a march on Washington to build up the antiwar movement and, coincidentally, the New Left.

I am a believer in nonviolence including opposition to the institutional violence of our society. . . . I think we need profound economic change in this country but I have never at any time in my life belonged to a political organization. . . . I know we have Democrats, Republicans, Socialists and Communists in our organization and we are proud of the policy that we exclude no one.

The Pentagon march had the familiar range of participants from Jerry Rubin of Berkeley, a member of the pro–Red China Progessive Labor Party and leader of the Youth International Party (Yippies), to traditional pacifists. Marchers included antiwar celebrities such as Dr. Benjamin Spock, eminent baby doctor, the Reverend William Sloan Coffin, chaplain of Yale University, and writers Norman Mailer and Robert Lowell.

Their different philosophies caused a clash between the militant leftists and the old-line pacifists. A member of Rubin's militant Berkeley group was named editor of the march committee's publication. A predemonstration issue promised: "We will fill hallways and block the entrances [of the Pentagon]. Thousands of people will disrupt the center of the American war machine. In the name of humanity we will call the warmakers to task."

That militant statement upset the pacifists, who intended doing nothing of the kind. They protested and the issue was scrapped. A new, less militant editor was appointed.

The clash within the march organization did not deter the militants, once the demonstration was under way. On the grounds of the Pentagon, attempts were made to crash through troops blocking entrances. Tear gas went off in the crowd, though all sides denied using it. By the time the demonstration ended, 202 persons had been arrested.

The number of participants in the march could only be estimated. The Communist Party newspaper, the *Daily World*, put the number at 200,000. Washington Police Chief John Layton set it at 55,000 while the Pentagon gave the number as 35,000.

Among the extremists of the New Left, antiwar views were mixed with heavy doses of anti-Americanism. A group called the U.S. Committee to Aid the National Liberation Front [Vietcong]

Antiwar demonstrations, such as this two-mile march from the Lincoln Memorial (background) to the Pentagon, keep feeding the flames of opposition to both the war and the "establishment," and provide occasions for dramatic get-togethers of leftists from all parts of the country.

of South Vietnam distributed a pamphlet at one antiwar rally which urged people to "show your opposition to the U.S. government's aggression by expressing your support for the Vietnamese people's fight in defense of their liberty. . . . The peace movement must come out in support of the NLF [National Liberation Front]. The peace movement should work to show that the real 'enemy' of Americans is not in Vietnam but here in our own country."

Another of the more militant groups has been the Vietnam Day Committee (VDC). Among its founders was Jerry Rubin. Based in Berkeley, the committee has been extremely active in a variety of protest activities, including distribution among troops of antiwar literature, attempts to block troop trains, and innumerable

Screaming performances, combined with provocation of troops guarding the Pentagon, also serve to produce publicity photographs of this kind and thereby promote the New Left.

protest marches in which its members are usually the ones carrying Vietcong flags.

Many VDC members were among the supporters of Ronald
Ramsey, known to U.S. troops in Vietnam as Granny Goose, an
American whose antiwar message is broadcast by Radio Hanoi.
Ramsey lived in California before he fled the country.

An example of VDC propaganda is contained in this excerpt
from a pamphlet passed out to soldiers: "You may soon be sent
to Vietnam. . . . You have a right to know as much about this war
as anyone. After all, it's you—not your congressman—who might
get killed." The pamphlet goes on to say:

> As far as the Vietnamese are concerned, we are fighting on
> the side of Hitlerism! and they hope we lose. . . . When the
> South Vietnamese people see you in your foreign uniform, they
> will think of you as their enemy. You are the ones bombing their
> towns. . . . We believe that the entire war in Vietnam is criminal
> and immoral. We believe that the atrocities which are neces-
> sary to wage this war against the people of Vietnam are inex-
> cusable. We hope that you, too, find yourself, as a human being,
> unable to tolerate this nightmare war and we hope that you
> will oppose it. . . . A growing number of GIs have already refused
> to fight in Vietnam and have been court-martialed. They have
> shown great courage.

Antiwar sentiment has appeared in the ranks of the military.
The initial reaction of commanders was harsh. A series of courts-
martial handed down stiff sentences. But then at higher levels
it apparently was decided that local commanders were overreact-
ing. Orders went out to base commanders reminding them that
troops "have both civil rights and military obligations" and pointing out that regulations permit soldiers to participate in legal
antiwar demonstrations so long as they are off duty and out of
uniform.

The army also amended its regulations to make it clear that
"military personnel are entitled to the same free access to pub-
lications as are other citizens . . . except in cases where a publica-

tion constitutes a clear danger to military loyalty, discipline or morale."

The Democratic National Convention in Chicago in September 1968 gave the New Left an exceptional opportunity for protest, confrontation, and maximum public exposure. The party of President Lyndon Johnson was going to nominate its candidate for president. That event would be covered by thousands of newsmen and television cameras.

The result was the most violent and best publicized of all the antiwar demonstrations. Throughout the convention week there were bloody clashes between demonstrators and police. Millions of Americans sat appalled before their television sets watching convention hall scenes alternate with scenes of street violence.

Long after the convention ended the controversy continued over who had been to blame for the violence. One study placed much of the blame on the authorities and called it a "police riot." Others defended the police and blamed the demonstrators for deliberately provoking clashes.

Both sides had prepared long in advance. Extra police and troops were brought to Chicago to deal with any outbreaks of violence. Security at the convention hall was so tight that many delegates became angry at the trouble involved simply in entering the hall.

As for the antiwar group, as early as November 16, 1967, Jerry Rubin had written: "See you next August in Chicago at the Democratic National Convention. Bring pot, fake delegates' cards, smoke bombs, costumes, blood to throw, and all kinds of interesting props. Also football helmets."

The following June, Dellinger and Hayden told a news conference in New York: "We are planning tactics of prolonged direct action to put heat on the government and its political party. We realize that it will be no picnic, but responsibility for any violence that develops lies with the authorities, not the demonstrators."

Inside the hall, the convention spotlighted some of the divisions within the Democratic Party. The violence in the streets pointed up a basic split among the leftist groups in the antiwar movement. After the week of violence, there was some soul searching

Jerry Rubin, leader of the Yippies, arrives in Washington with his beard, bare chest, and toy M-16 rifle to pursue his tactic of using ridicule to undermine the "establishment."

on the left. Tom Hayden stayed in Chicago and addressed a rally in Grant Park, scene of some of the bloodiest convention week clashes. "It may well be," he said, "that the era of organized, peaceful and orderly demonstrations is coming to an end and that other methods will be needed."

Rubin's group, the Yippies, had been a popular target of police and television cameramen. But the wild appearing Yippies with their beards, long hair, and beads seemed just as offensive to the old-line, disciplined Communist Party members as they were to Mayor Richard J. Daley.

Julius Lester, a leader of SNCC, defended the Yippies in an article in the far-left *National Guardian:*

Eruption of violence during the Democratic National Convention at Chicago, regardless of the cause, played into the hands of the Old and the New Left by creating the impression with photographs of this kind that the United States is a police state.

Smug, self-righteous, New Left ideologies limply put down the Yippies for being politically immature and irresponsible. Those of us who involve ourselves in more overt political action have no guarantee to the truth, but because we are trying to follow in the footsteps of Lenin, Mao and Fidel, we arrogantly think we do. This is America. Not Russia, China and Cuba, and in America, maybe, just maybe, the paths to revolution will be clothed not only in guerrilla uniforms but beads and incense.

The techniques used by communists are now familiar to students of communism. Sanger defines one used at the Pentagon demonstration as "breaking images." He describes it as "picturing the

A Yippie loudly at work at the time of the Democratic Party convention in Chicago, where 2,500 Yippies gathered to make their contribution to the tumult.

police as brutal; soldiers as blood-thirsty, stupid louts with bayonets; and the government as heartless seekers after power. This technique of making police look like Cossacks is an old Bolshevik gambit."

He gave this example, a familiar scene at mass demonstrations:

> For instance, take the activists, the men and women trained for action. They are told to go and sit, perhaps to pray, outside a cathedral or on the pavement in front of the Lincoln Memorial, or other shrine, wherever they know the police will have to shove them aside. Because they refuse to budge, they force the police to move in. They are taught to "go limp" and be dragged along. And when they are put in the paddy wagon, they must struggle and fight for the benefit of the press and camera men. What emerges is a story or a picture of an 18-year-old boy or girl struggling and being beaten over the head. If he is injured that's fine; he must make certain that the press sees how badly he is hurt.

Another technique is to distribute little plastic bags of red ink which demonstrators can break over their heads, creating a picture of bloodied youth, the victim of police brutality.

Such techniques created sympathy, especially among young people. These techniques did not start with the Pentagon demonstration. They had been in use since the first antiwar demonstrations early in 1965. They helped turn many young people against the authorities.

Arguments such as those made by Carl Oglesby, president of SDS, at an antiwar rally in 1965, also helped the communist cause. To Oglesby, the Vietnam war was "a revolution, as honest a revolution as you can find anywhere in history." American involvement was described in traditional Marxist terms: "to safeguard ... American interests around the world against revolution or revolutionary change."

Every effort is made to picture the United States as the villain in its relations with the world, particularly the underdeveloped countries.

Antiwar protesters are dispersed by police after burning draft cards near the Supreme Court Building following a ruling that burning and mutilating draft cards is illegal.

The draft gave SDS one of its first big campus issues. In the spring of 1966, General Lewis B. Hershey, selective service director, announced plans to draft some college students. Two criteria would be used: a student's standing in class, and his performance on a Selective Service Qualification Test.

The announcement created a furor on campuses. The SDS demanded that universities refuse to cooperate by giving student grades to the military. At the University of Chicago, SDS led a demonstration in which students seized control of the administra-

Making their position crystal-clear for onlookers, young demonstrators carry the Vietcong flag (left) and the flag of North Vietnam (center) during their own "counterinaugural" parade in Washington, January 1968.

tion building and held it for three days. It was the first such building takeover by students. Other demonstrations occurred at the University of Wisconsin, City College of New York, and Oberlin College in Ohio. At last, SDS had an issue with which it could muster widespread support from moderate students.

The use of napalm in Vietnam gave the New Left still another issue that helped it win support from moderates. Stories began appearing in the press about the horrible burns suffered by Vietnamese civilians as a result of napalm dropped on villages. SDS quickly mobilized large-scale campus demonstrations aimed at recruiters from Dow Chemical Company, manufacturer of napalm. At Harvard, an angry crowd of students held a recruiter captive in a building for several hours.

Other SDS targets were ROTC programs and defense research. Protests aimed at specific, narrow targets began to have effect. University officials began to reexamine ROTC and some of their research activities. Some stopped giving credit for ROTC; others changed the program from a required to a voluntary one. Many schools announced their intention to turn down classified defense research contracts. In a parallel reaction, the Pentagon began declassifying many of its research projects.

A major goal of the left wing of the antiwar movement had been to forge an alliance with the civil rights movement. The New and Old Left had long attacked the war not only as a manifestation of capitalism but also of racism. There were economic arguments that turned some civil rights leaders against the war. The United States was spending billions of dollars each year in Vietnam, money that many people thought should be spent to fight poverty at home.

Thus, Martin Luther King, Jr., became increasingly critical of the war. He began taking part in major antiwar demonstrations. In a speech in New York on April 4, 1967, King called the start of the Johnson administration's war on poverty "a shining moment." It seemed, he said, as if—

there was a real promise of hope for the poor—both black and white—through the poverty program. Then came the buildup

Student radicals stage a sit-in at Marquette University, Milwaukee, providing a vivid example of the "politics of confrontation."

In still another campus protest, a demonstrator points a toy gun at a Marine recruiter leaving the campus of Oberlin College. Ohio.

in Vietnam and I watched the program broken and eviscerated as if it were some idle political plaything of a society gone mad on war and I knew that America would never invest the necessary funds or energies in rehabilitation of its poor so long as Vietnam continued to draw men and skills and money like some demonic, destructive suction tube.

In late 1965, SNCC became the first major civil rights organization to declare its opposition to U.S. involvement in Vietnam. SNCC was then moving farther left and toward exclusion of whites from its ranks. It played on the theme that Vietnam was a war between a powerful white nation and a poor nonwhite country. It issued a statement accusing the government of being "deceptive in its claims of concern for the freedom of the Vietnamese people, just as the government has been deceptive in claiming concern for the freedom of colored people in such other countries as the Dominican Republic, the Congo, South Africa, Rhodesia and in the United States itself."

The different devices and issues exploited by the communists, usually in conjunction with various elements of the New Left, include the following:

• Mass protests. The New Left was instrumental in organizing mass demonstrations of opposition to the war. One of the first such demonstrations was the April 1965 Student March on Washington called by SDS.

• University teach-ins. One of the earliest methods used to publicize arguments against the war was to recruit scholars to participate in teach-ins. Normally, such teach-ins consisted of endless denunciations of U.S. policy. Occasionally they took the form of debates with some faculty members supporting the administration position.

• Demonstrations against university involvement in any military activities. These were aimed particularly at ROTC programs, military and Central Intelligence Agency recruiters, and Defense Research.

• The Antidraft movement. Resistance to the draft, either by refusal to show up for induction, claiming conscientious objector status, or burning one's draft card, became part of the antiwar movement. Another part of draft resistance was the effort to shut down induction centers with mass demonstrations.

• Linking the antiwar and civil rights movements.

Many ask how effective the communists and the New Left actually have been with their demonstrations and violent behavior, on and off the campus.

In private, communists reply: "Didn't LBJ renounce his hopes to another term in the White House? And didn't Nixon start withdrawing U.S. troops from Vietnam, in a basic shift of U.S. policy? And didn't we have quite a lot to do with all that?"

These rhetorical replies provide food for thought.

Chapter Three

How They Exploit Blacks

Soon after leading the Bolsheviks to power in Russia in 1917, V.I. Lenin pointed to the American Negroes as constituting an "oppressed class" which should be most helpful in extending the communist revolution to the United States.

Here was a large body of American citizens, bursting with grievances, apparently ripe for joining almost any revolutionary movement. Lenin evidently envisaged the Negroes in the United States flocking to join the Communist Party, and in 1921, just two years after creation of the party in the United States, he is reported to have been annoyed with its leaders for failing to exploit the opportunities he saw.

From that time onward, the Communist Party has been working ceaselessly on the black population in the United States.

It began by preaching the class struggle as set forth in the economic teachings of Karl Marx. It explained to any Negro who would listen that racial discrimination was only part of a broader picture—the picture of the working class, composed of all races and "exploited" equally by the capitalist class.

However, this appeal to a "class" of workers who were being equally "victimized" by another "class" didn't seem to make much sense to the Negro. He could understand a "class" of blacks being exploited by whites, but he couldn't quite see how a white, who called himself a communist, would be in a position to do much for a black. There was, after all, an important difference in color, and the black was convinced that his problem was a color problem.

If the whites had a class problem involving differences between "capitalists" and the "proletariat," then that was a white problem, which seemed to have little or nothing to do with the black problem.

All this created a most difficult situation for the predominantly white Communist Party in the United States, and it is no less difficult today than it was in the early 1920s when Lenin was prodding his comrades to bring the black population of the United States under the red banner.

Instead of flocking to the Communist Party, it seemed at one time that the blacks would join the "Back to Africa" movement launched by Marcus Garvey. Communist headquarters in Moscow could not tolerate such an idea. From a communist viewpoint, "Back to Africa" amounted to running away from the problem in the United States instead of staying there to fight, together with the communists, to bring about another communist revolution. Accordingly, the communists, anxious not to lose potentially valuable allies, waged a campaign against Garvey and his "escapist" movement.

When Cyril V. Briggs came along with his African Blood Brotherhood, dedicated to the idea of establishing a separate black nation within the borders of the United States, the communists had another problem in deciding what position to take. Here again the blacks were thinking in terms of race rather than "class struggle." Nevertheless, in this case the blacks would remain in the United States, and the communists, by supporting the Brotherhood, could draw some of them into the Communist Party.

Expediency influenced the decision, and the communists lent their support to the idea of a separate black state. In exchange, they were able to work on and eventually convert some of the Blood Brotherhood to the communist cause.

The idea of separation of blacks from whites versus the concept of integration of blacks in a predominantly white country gave rise to an issue which continues to divide blacks to this day. And this issue, for the Communist Party, represents a hot potato which it

With the singing of the Star Spangled Banner, the Communist Party of the United States opens an annual convention in New York City and proceeds with its plans to overthrow the U.S. government—"peaceably" and "legally."

tosses from one hand to the other.

In 1958 the Communist Party turned its back on the black segregationists and came out quite firmly for the principle of integration. However, with the revival of the black segregation movement, this time under the auspices of such extremists as the Black Panthers, the communists tend to slide back and forth again, trying to catch allies wherever possible.

The problem for the Communist Party is complicated by the fact that it is subject to directives from Moscow. And Moscow, being many thousands of miles away, tends to adopt theoretical positions without understanding the facts and circumstances in the United States.

Benjamin Gitlow, twice a Communist Party candidate for vice president, described the effort put forth by the Soviets in his book, *I Confess.* With money sent by the Comintern, Gitlow wrote, the party—

> created a special Negro department, built special Negro organizations, issued Negro papers and periodicals, made every inducement for Negroes to join the party, took advantage of every opportunity to penetrate existing Negro organizations and to participate in Negro movements, for the purpose of bringing its program before the Negro masses. . . . Yet in spite of our efforts and the large sums of money spent on that sort of propaganda, we made very little headway among the Negro masses. The Negroes in the United States refused to flock into the Communist Party and gave little credence to our promises.

Probably the most successful Communist effort to establish a working relationship with Negroes occurred in the 1930s with the formation of the National Negro Congress. For years, the communists had been attacking the National Association for the Advancement of Colored People (NAACP) and the Urban League as bourgeois organizations more interested in preserving capitalism than in helping the Negro worker.

The NAACP had rallied other Negro organizations to form a Joint Committee on National Recovery. Its purpose was to approach and work with New Deal agencies on projects to help Negroes recover from the depression. A bitter opponent of the communists, the NAACP did not invite communist organizations to participate. But there were communists and communist sympathizers among committee members. The committee, in turn, formed the National Negro Congress with A. Philip Randolph as its president. The Congress served as a public vehicle for the Negro leaders to make their views known to the Roosevelt administration.

A speech by Randolph to the Congress in 1937 gives a picture of its activities and also its political leanings. According to him, the Congress—

> marshalled militant black men to march in the van with the CIO to chalk up an enviable record in bringing workers into the field of industrial organization. . . . The Congress has brought eager and aggressive black youth to grapple with the problem of the organization of the tobacco workers in Virginia. . . . To the laundry workers in Washington, D.C., the Congress is carrying the message of trade union organization. . . . On the civil and political rights front, the Congress joined the fighting forces of the National Association for the Advancement of Colored People, to battle for the Wagner-Gavagan federal anti-lynching bill. . . .
>
> But not only has it fought in the front for the defense of the rights of the Negro people, the Congress has also thrown its might with the progressive forces in the land to aid in the cause of Spanish democracy, the independence of China from the dominance of Japan, and the restoration of Haile Selassie to an independent kingdom of Ethiopia.

The communists concentrated on capturing control of the National Negro Congress and by 1938 they had largely succeeded. Then came the Nazi-Soviet pact and suddenly the Congress was denouncing antifascist movements as imperialist. After driving Randolph and other anticommunists out of the Congress, the communist leadership set it on an antiwar campaign. With language that has changed little over the years, the Congress said the administration and its supporters "insult the Negro people by brazenly asking us to support this war in order that we may further enslave ourselves and oppressed peoples throughout the world."

A year later, when Hitler invaded the Soviet Union, the Congress began calling for all-out prosecution of the war against fascism. By then the Congress had lost whatever effectiveness it ever had as a communist front.

The development of the civil rights movement and the long, drawn-out war in Vietnam opened new possibilities for the communists. They played on the theme that the war was diverting billions of dollars from worthy causes at home—notably, a massive program to raise the blacks from poverty and the ghetto. In a bid for favor with black nationalists, the communists also lent support to the charge that the war in Vietnam was "racist"—the white American versus the Oriental.

However, in trying to exploit both the war and the civil rights movement, the communists found themselves caught between two important black groups—moderates and extremists.

Moderate Negro leaders, such as those of the NAACP, were not taken in by communist agitation on behalf of civil rights for blacks. These men already had long experience with communists, and they fully understood that communists were interested in civil rights not to help the black man but to help expand the power of the Communist Party and the influence of the Soviet Union.

They also saw exceptional cynicism in the fact that a communist country such as the Soviet Union, which denies civil rights within its own borders, should be such a champion of civil rights in other countries. Agitation for civil rights, as conducted by communists, seeks to discredit and undermine the established order. Should the communists come to power, there can be little doubt that they would soon do away with the civil rights for which they had been agitating so long and so hard.

Moderate Negroes, dedicated to the principle of integration and a solution of the black problem within the constitutional framework of the United States, also distrust the communist position on integration. The communists began to wobble again when a modern version of Garveyism appeared in the form of the Black Muslim movement.

Claude Lightfoot, one of the prominent Negro members of the Communist Party, criticized the Muslim movement by saying: "When it demeans everybody with a white face, when it glorifies everybody with a black face—then, clearly, it is out of touch with reality."

But he added: "Even their ultimate desire, a black-led republic within continental United States, if manifested by a large segment of the black community in socialist America, would be honored if American communists had anything to do with it."

Another reason why moderates prefer to have nothing to do with communists was clearly expressed by James Farmer when he said,

Claude Lightfoot, top-ranking Negro in the Communist Party of the United States, is found guilty in a Chicago court under the Smith Act, which makes it a crime to belong to an organization advocating violent overthrow of the U.S. government. The Smith Act later was declared unconstitutional, and Lightfoot is now free to go about the country preaching communism.

"A Negro finds it tough enough being black without being black *and* red."

The attitude of the black extremists is no less distasteful to the pro-Moscow communists of the United States. Their objection to these communists is that, for the most part, they are white and therefore should be treated as untouchables.

Since black extremists are segregationists, they cannot accept the communists when they pretend to favor integration.

Furthermore, the extremists, ready to embark on the most reckless schemes, including guerrilla warfare, consider themselves to be truly extreme and revolutionary. The pro-Soviet communists, on the other hand, appear to them to be "square," conservative, and reactionary. These communists uphold the Soviet line of coexistence with the predominantly white government of the United States. The black extremists refuse to "coexist" and say they are dedicated to bringing down the established order.

As Marxists, they prefer to be identified with those of Red China and North Vietnam. The latter may not be black, but they are not white, either.

This leaves the orthodox, pro-Soviet Communist Party in the position of waiting until the extremists cool off and a new opportunity should present itself for joining them. In the meantime, the communists may feel that the black extremists, to the extent that they weaken the established order, are doing some of their work for them.

To what extent are black extremists genuinely interested in civil rights for the black man?

Public statements issued by such men as Stokely Carmichael of SNCC, Eldridge Cleaver of the Black Panthers, and Floyd McKissick of CORE, indicate that their primary interest is a political one —to bring down the established order. They are not interested in civil rights that come through a peaceful settlement between blacks and whites based on the principle of integration.

It is on this basic point that moderates like Roy Wilkins of the NAACP and Whitney M. Young of the Urban League part company with the extremist leaders.

The moderate leaders warn that the course of violence and revolution advocated by the champions of "black power" would serve only to damage the hopes of the great majority of black Americans to be integrated into society on a basis of equality.

This view leads to the conclusion that the extremists are prepared to sacrifice civil rights in their pursuit of political, revolutionary goals.

Immediately after his election as chairman of SNCC in May 1966, Carmichael turned his group sharply to the left and toward a radical position. His subsequent moves abroad disclosed the nature of his interests.

He flew to Puerto Rico in January 1967, and there entered into relations with Castro supporters agitating for Puerto Rican independence from the United States.

Stokely Carmichael (left), "Black Power" leader now in exile, talks to Troung Chinh of communist Vietnam, during a visit to Hanoi.

He went to Cuba to confer directly with Fidel Castro and other leaders of the only communist state in the Western Hemisphere. In Havana he declared Castro to be "a source of inspiration."

He said that "we are moving toward urban guerrilla warfare within the United States."

He explained to a cheering crowd that "we have to fight in the United States in order to change the structure of that capitalist society. . . . We have no alternative but to use aggressive, armed violence."

In Hanoi, Carmichael said, "American Negroes in the United States give their total support to the Vietnamese people in their struggle against American imperialism."

Later, in Paris, he said, "We don't want peace in Vietnam. We want the Vietnamese to defeat the United States of America, and we think our blood is not too high a price to pay."

Carmichael's anti-American speeches around the world brought demands that action be taken against him if he returned to the United States. It also raised questions of how closely he was tied to the communists.

J. Edgar Hoover, in testimony before a House committee, said, "In espousing his philosophy of black power, Carmichael has been in frequent contact with Max Stanford, field chairman of the Revolutionary Action Movement (RAM), a highly secret, all-Negro, Marxist-Leninist Chinese Communist oriented organization which

Maxwell Stanford, director of U.S. operations for RAM, was also the founder of a Black Panther Party in New York City, August 1966.

advocates guerrilla warfare to obtain its goals." Hoover also described RAM as "dedicated to the overthrow of the capitalist system."

Speaking in Chicago in March 1968, Carmichael denied he was a communist and, as if to prove his point, shouted, "Communism is white." He told the same audience that "the world is dividing along color lines and proof of this was the meeting between Premier Kosygin and President Johnson. They got together and widened the split between Russia and China."

In a speech in Atlanta in December 1968, he talked about his conception of a new society as "free of racism and capitalism" but then added: "That does not mean it would be communism or socialism. That would be a problem of economics."

He repeated his calls for violence. "Don't pray for power," he told an audience at Mobile, Alabama. "Don't beg for power. Take it with a gun barrel."

Carmichael's denial that he is a communist recalls similar denials once made by Castro. There is still some argument on whether Fidel Castro formally was a communist at the time he took power in Havana. Most observers now agree that this is a technical point. What matters is that, once having gained power, he formed an alliance with the Soviet Union and converted Cuba into a communist state.

It is quite possible that, given the opportunity, men like Carmichael and Cleaver, both now operating in exile abroad, would follow a similar course.

Cleaver, who fled from California for allegedly violating his parole, first took refuge in Cuba. There a peculiar estrangement occurred.

Raymond Johnson, a Panther who reached Cuba by hijacking an airliner, told an American newsman that the black American exiles were unhappy in Havana. "We would like this information to reach the Black Panther Party in the United States," Johnson said, "so the party will know the unrevolutionary way we are being treated. . . . We think there's racial discrimination in Cuba."

According to reports, Cleaver, Johnson, and fellow Panthers were kept in isolation, cut off from the Cubans. One theory is that Castro

Eldridge Cleaver, a fugitive leader of the Black Panthers, speaks to Algerians and Palestinian Arabs at a news conference in Algiers on the occasion of opening a Black Panther liaison office there. Cleaver said his movement backs the Arabs' "liberation struggle" against Israel.

could not let Cleaver move about Cuba, preaching racism and calling on blacks to overthrow the whites and seize power. Castro, of course, is white.

Another theory is that the Soviet Union, holding a dominant position in Havana, was not pleased with Cleaver's presence since the leader of the Black Panthers was more partial to Peking (nonwhite) than to Moscow (predominantly white).

At any rate, Cleaver moved to Algeria and continued directing the Panthers' revolutionary activity from there.

J. Edgar Hoover describes the Panthers as the most violent of all black militant groups: "They are recruiting known criminals and

Robert Williams, black revolutionary leader, returns to the United States to face kidnapping charges after eight years of exile in Cuba, Red China, and Africa.

hoodlums and encouraging them to engage in a broad range of ter-
rorist tactics and other criminal actions while explaining that such
actions, being revolutionary in nature, are justified."

The pro-Moscow Communist Party in the United States, concerned about the course on which the black extremists had
embarked, tried to slow them down. Claude Lightfoot, the high-
ranking Negro member of the Communist Party, sounded this
warning:

"Can it be successfully argued that an armed struggle in present
conditions in the United States would enjoy the active or passive
support by anything like a majority of the American people? Clearly
not. Under such circumstances, the resort to arms of an offensive
nature could only lead to suicide."

However, warnings of this kind did not deter the Panthers and
did not win any of their sympathy for the pro-Moscow Communist
Party. Therefore, the party shifted its position again. Early in
1969, the Communist Party's Commission on Black Liberation
voted to support the Black Panther Party program, to work closely
with the Panthers, and to join them if permitted to do so.

Notwithstanding such courting, the Panthers and other black
extremists continue to identify themselves with the communists of
Peking rather than those of Moscow.

Whether it is one or the other, the result may be the same for
the great majority of black Americans. Their leaders are convinced
that violence and alliances with foreign powers are more likely
to delay than to promote the integration of blacks in American
society.

Chapter Four

How They Exploit Disorder

Revolutionaries thrive on chaos. To the extremists of the American left, determined to bring about a revolution, the big city riots of recent summers offered an opportunity not to be ignored. In nearly every disturbance, the trained agitators of the far left appeared on the scene.

Their goal: inflame passions, incite violence, foment disorder, all in the hope that violence would lead to more violence, until, in large areas of our cities, authority would be undermined and the government would be viewed by many of its citizens as an enemy. For it is in such conditions that revolutionary movements can grow and, perhaps, succeed.

Is there a chance that what happened in Cuba and Algeria could happen here? It is possible, according to some authorities: patterns that have led to such revolutions elsewhere are being repeated here.

Part of that pattern is frustration. Political violence begins with a grievance, which is sometimes genuine, sometimes phony.

And when that frustration leads to violence, extremists are on hand to exploit it. It happened in Harlem.

The incident that touched off the Harlem riot was the shooting of a 16-year-old Negro named James Powell by an off-duty white police lieutenant, Thomas R. Gilligan. The police officer said the boy lunged at him with a knife and he shot in self-defense. A grand jury later found the lieutenant innocent of any criminal liability.

There were elements in the incident that inflamed feelings bred by real and imagined grievances within the Negro community. For years extremists had bombarded the community with cries of police brutality. It was a standard charge made by extremists of the left as well as black nationalist groups, all of whom were determined to undermine the power of authorities in the Negro community.

Into that atmosphere came the case of the 122-pound Negro youth shot to death by a 200-pound white police officer.

Two days after the shooting a protest rally was held. Speakers demanded that action be taken against Gilligan. A crowd began marching from the rally to a police station, two blocks away. There, they were met by a line of helmeted police officers. Bottles and bricks were thrown at the police who then fired shots over the heads of the marchers. It was to be six days before the city would be calm again. Rioting, looting, and burning erupted in Negro neighborhoods throughout the city as well as in nearby cities.

What role did communists and other extremists of the left have in that rioting? Many of those who believed that the police officer had acted wrongly or could have avoided killing the boy were not communists or extremists.

But it was an incident that could easily be exploited by extremists, and they wasted little time in doing so.

The Progressive Labor Party, the Harlem Defense Council, and the Community Action on Housing were quick to call for violence. All three groups were placed under a court order barring them from further agitation.

No sooner had trouble broken out in Harlem than William Epton, a Negro member of the pro-Chinese Progressive Labor Party, took to the streets to try to stir crowds to violence. "We will not be fully free until we smash this state completely," Epton shouted.

Epton later was indicted and convicted of inciting to riot.

The Progressive Labor Party did its best to encourage violence. It was among those who circulated posters reading: "Wanted for Murder—Gilligan the Cop." The party newspaper, *Challenge*, edi-

In the wake of the assassination of Martin Luther King, Jr., looting, rioting, and fires break out in the heart of Harlem, the Negro settlement of New York City.

William Epton, center, active in the Maoist Progressive Labor Party, links arms with associates as he prepares to lead an antipolice parade in Harlem. He was arrested soon afterward.

torialized during the rioting as follows:

> The rebellion sparked by his murder [Powell's] will not end
> soon—in fact, indications are that it is spreading throughout the
> city. . . . There are reds in Harlem, yes—black reds. Bill Epton
> and the PLP have never made a secret of their revolutionary posi-
> tion, neither has *Challenge*. We advocate and work for a people's
> revolution to establish socialism, with all power in the hands of
> working people. This is the only permanent solution to Jim Crow,
> unemployment and killer-cops.

And the Harlem Defense Council distributed leaflets calling on
Harlem residents to "organize your blocks." The leaflets said, "The
Harlem Defense Council calls on all black people of Harlem to set
up block committees with the purpose of defending each and every
block in Harlem from the cops."

The minutes of a postriot meeting of Progressive Labor's National
Coordinating Committee quoted party chairman Milton Rosen as
saying, "When I talk about revolution, what I mean is that you want
to overthrow the system and have the dictatorship of the proletariat."

The minutes also quoted another committee member as complain-
ing that "we didn't get the support we needed and could have got-
ten even from the East Side Club [of the party]."

As for the pro-Moscow Communist Party, it spent the period of
the Harlem riot denying it had any connection with it and pointing
the finger at the pro-Peking Progressive Labor Party, which it
termed "parasites in the Negro freedom movement." Communist
Party leaders also emphasized that they had expelled the pro-
Chinese extremists from their party.

But Soviet-style communists are not as innocent of promoting
disorder as the Communist Party-U.S.A. would like people to
believe. Sanger, for example, cites his personal experience in the
Soviet Union in 1933 and 1934:

> When I graduated from the Harvard Business School I decided
> to go into the Foreign Service. But I couldn't make up my mind
> about what was going on in Russia—was it good or was it not?

So I contacted Socialists and Communists. I didn't know this at the time, but they put me on the "fellow traveler conveyer-belt." This is meant to help an interested student get around in Russia—make it easy for him or her to see things there and bring him out a fellow traveler.

Sanger says the system still operates. One of the things he attended was a series of lectures on how to foment revolution. "The communists have been training troublemakers for decades," he said.

Sanger's experience in the Soviet Union gave him insights into how communists are trained to view mob violence and exploit it. "To us, a mob is a mob. To the communists, a mob is three pieces," he said:

First of all there are the minutemen—people you can get into the streets fast. For example, any time you want to start a riot in Latin America, you can get the students out fast, often on something quite unrelated to your real objective.

The second element is the street fillers—the large numbers. In an Arab country they may be the refugees. In Europe, they may be the unemployed. On a campus, they may be perennial students. But, in themselves, these groups do no more than just mill around.

This is where the action groups come in—and you can spot them easily. They are the third and smallest element, but they give direction to the rest of the mob.

Were these factors present in riots in American cities? Sanger was in Washington during the eruption following the assassination of Dr. Martin Luther King, Jr., in April 1968. "I could see gangs starting to move around picking up followers," he said. "Mostly they were teen-agers, but they were led by older persons—tough-looking types in their mid-20s or even older. It was these leaders, who, as far as I could see, later smashed the first windows and then stepped aside and let others do the damage."

He pointed to the presence in Washington of extremists such as Stokely Carmichael: "You get various reports of what he was up

Cover of a pamphlet reportedly circulated by SNCC, calling on blacks to organize a revolution against whites.

to. What is known is that Carmichael was in Havana last summer [1967] and I don't think he was just sitting in the sun. He also was in Prague in July and in Hanoi in August."

After the first night of rioting in the nation's capital, Carmichael held a news conference. In a widely reported statement, he said, "The only way to survive is to get some guns. Because that's the only way White America keeps us in check, because she's got the guns."

It was not the first time Carmichael had made statements that appeared designed to instigate violence. On his overseas travels he was quoted in Havana and Hanoi as calling on American Negroes to carry on urban guerrilla warfare.

Nearly one year before the Washington riots, Carmichael had appeared on the scene of a tense confrontation in Atlanta between a Negro crowd and city police. Carmichael then urged the crowd to "take to the streets and force the police department to work until they drop in their tracks."

But both in Washington and Atlanta, Carmichael's words were ignored. There were no serious shooting incidents in Washington. In Atlanta the crowd eventually listened to community leaders who urged residents to go home. Many residents of the area later signed a petition urging Carmichael to leave town.

In addition to their efforts to create more trouble once disorder has broken out, extremists of the left have played a role in establishing an atmosphere in which trouble is likely to occur. We saw that one factor in the Harlem riot was the impact that cries of "police brutality" had on people over a number of years.

J. Edgar Hoover discussed this point in an appearance before a House Committee:

The cumulative effect of almost 50 years of Communist Party activity in the United States cannot be minimized, for it has contributed to disrupting race relations in this country and has exerted an insidious effect on the life and times of our nation. As a prime example, for years it has been communist policy to charge "police brutality" in a calculated campaign to discredit law enforcement and to accentuate racial issues.

The riots and disorders of the past three years clearly high-
light the success of this communist smear campaign in popular-
izing the cry of "police brutality" to the point where it has
been accepted by many individuals having no affiliation or
sympathy for the communist movement.

Mayor Sam Yorty of Los Angeles referred to the same issue in
discussing communist activity before and after the rioting in the
Watts section of his city. Yorty told a congressional committee
that known communists had been promoting the police brutality
issue in Los Angeles for many years. "For some time there has
existed a world-wide subversive campaign to stigmatize all police
as brutal," the mayor said. "The cry of police brutality has been
shouted in cities all over the world by communists, dupes and
demagogues irrespective of the facts."

An example of this propaganda was a list of demands issued by
the Progressive Labor Party after the Watts riots. They included:
"1. Arrest the Nazi Police Chief Parker, Governor Brown and
Mayor Yorty and bring them to trial for murder. 2. Disarm the
criminal police and punish the guilty ones."

One of the bloodiest riots in American history erupted in
Newark, New Jersey, in the summer of 1967. The Newark riot
lasted six days, and 23 people were killed.

The pattern in Newark was a familiar one. John Smith, a
Negro cab driver, was arrested on a charge of driving with a
revoked license. He was taken to police headquarters and rumors
quickly spread through the Negro community that he had been
killed by police. A special commission, appointed by the governor
of New Jersey, investigated the riot and found widespread distrust of the police and city administration among the Negro
community. There were forces working within Newark to exploit
and spread that distrust.

There was, for example, LeRoi Jones, antiwhite Negro play-
wright. A resident of Newark, Jones is noted for the bitterly
antiwhite tone of his writing.

There was also the Newark Community Union Project, sponsored by Students for a Democratic Society and led by Tom

Smoke pours from gutted buildings which were destroyed in a night of rioting in Cleveland's eastside district in the summer of 1968. At least 10 persons were killed, 3 of them police officers.

Part of the nation's capital is set afire during Negro rioting in the spring of 1968.

Hayden. This project, along with others set up in other cities, represented SDS's first serious effort to extend beyond the campus. SDS members moved into poor neighborhoods and tried to organize the residents to give them the power to help improve conditions in their areas. In theory it has the potential for being a novel and worthwhile approach to solving some urban problems.

However, the methods used by SDS often were very similar to the disruptive tactics they employed on campuses. An article in *Studies on the Left,* an SDS publication, described the tactics: "At every level, NCUP disrupts; it challenges hollow democratic rhetoric, it challenges authority. As its members continually pursue the question of who should control various programs and agencies, who should make decisions, who should receive benefits, what is the nature of representation, it challenges the bases on which power is legitimatized in this society."

Captain Charles Kinney of the Newark Police Department described the incident that touched off rioting as "spontaneously brought about by the hot, humid weather, together with the climate that had been created in the city by racists and subversives."

Kinney added that "it is believed also that certain individuals and groups were looking for just such an incident to trigger a disturbance, and were prepared to act decisively when it occurred."

Hayden, a leader of the New Left, who has been at the scene of many disorders including the Columbia University riots and the clashes at the Democratic National Convention in 1968, later described the revolutionary potential of the Newark ghetto in a book, *Rebellion in Newark:* "This is not a time for radical illusions about revolution. Stagnancy and conservatism are essential facts of ghetto life. It undoubtedly is true that most Negroes desire the comfort and security that white people possess. There is little revolutionary consciousness or commitment to violence per se in the ghetto."

An example of how SDS operated in Newark is described by Jesse Allen, an SDS organizer, in an article on a campaign for tenement repairs. Writing in *Studies on the Left,* Allen said:

We complained to City Hall. . . . We did not get any coop-

eration from our mayor and the landlords just wouldn't fix up.
So some of us got together and started talking and we decided
to form a block committee.... We organized eight blocks in
our neighborhood in about six weeks.... We decided to go
on a rent strike.... When the landlords came around for the
rent we told them we're not paying any more rent to them.
We had their money, but we're putting it into the bank until
they fixed the houses.

Newark fits well into the pattern described by Sanger in discussing insurrection. "In the classic pattern," he said, "are the
efforts by the aggrieved to get action, first through peaceful dele-
gations, then through quiet demonstrations, and then through
nuisance demonstrations.... Unless the discontented get dramatic
and speedy results, I think a lot more of them are going to
decide the answer is: 'Burn, baby, burn!' Extremists in this country will encourage such escalation."

One way to escalate violence is to work within organizations
that are trying to achieve change through demonstrations. Sanger
describes such a potential situation:

They have gone as far as they dare and they don't know
what to do. Then somebody gets up at the back of the hall—
an activist possibly, and probably a "sleeping communist"—
and says: "Friends, you can't overturn this government sitting
in the streets. That's ridiculous. The only way to do it is by
real violence...!" The first thing you know, this communist is on
the central committee; the next thing, he's guiding the show.

Bayard Rustin, the Negro civil rights leader who organized
the 1963 March on Washington, tells a story that illustrates one
attitude toward violence. In an article in the *Journal of Inter-
group Relations*, Rustin told of an encounter he and Martin
Luther King, Jr., had when they walked through Watts not long
after the riot. Rustin wrote:

A young man in Watts said to me and Dr. King, "You know,

we won."

I said, "What do you mean, you won?"

He said, "They finally listened to our manifesto." And he kept talking about the manifesto.

And I said, "Young man, what do you mean by the manifesto? Would you mind letting me and Dr. King see a copy of it?"

He pulled out a match box; he pulled out a single match; he lit it. He said, "Daddy, that was our manifesto, and the slogan was Burn, baby, burn."

I said, "But you haven't told me how you won."

He said, "Well, I'll tell you how we won. We were four years telling these white folks peacefully what we needed. We asked them to come and talk with us. They didn't come. We tried to get some war on poverty. It didn't come. But after our manifesto daddy, the mayor, the governor, you, Dr. King, everybody came."

Harlem, Watts, Newark: these and other disorders were the subject of investigation by federal and state commissions as well as by police and the FBI. All dealt with the question of leftist influence. But there was little agreement.

All recognized that communists and other extremists were busy trying to inflame passions. How successful their efforts were or what role they played in initiating violence is the issue in question.

Captain Kinney, for example, cites leftist efforts to destroy confidence in the police department through the issue of police brutality. A special commission appointed by Governor Richard J. Hughes studied the New Jersey riots and cited grand jury criticism of the police department for political interference as well as the employment of a public relations director who was also working for a major figure in organized crime in New Jersey.

"There is a widespread belief in the Negro community," said the commission, "that these grand jury presentments were true. Compounding it is the visible evidence in the Negro area of gambling and vice."

Attending a four-day conference on Black Power in Newark, New Jersey, are (seated from left) comedian Dick Gregory; Ron Karenga, leader of the Black Nationalist Cultural Organization of the United States; Rap Brown, national chairman of the Student National Coordinating Committee (SNCC); and Ralph Featherstone of SNCC.

Also cited was the lack of communication between the city administration and Negro community. Prior to the riot, bitter disputes had been going on over the location of a medical school and the appointment of a new secretary for the school. The site proposed for the medical school was in a Negro neighborhood, and many residents opposed it because it would displace many families. The school board controversy arose over plans to appoint a white man with no college education as city councilman rather than a Negro certified public accountant. Hayden and his SDS organizers were actively arousing opposition in both disputes.

The commission report said the city administration "did not adequately realize the bitterness in important sectors of the Negro community" over the two issues.

A commission chaired by John McCone, former head of the Central Intelligence Agency, studied the Watts riot and concluded: "There is no reliable evidence of outside leadership or pre-established plans for the rioting."

Evelle J. Younger, Los Angeles County district attorney, was asked about the activities in Watts of the Communist Party, and such extremist groups as the Black Panthers and the Revolutionary Action Movement. "They were distributing pamphlets," Younger said. "They have been distributing pamphlets since I got out of high school, and it would be a mistake, I think, to assume that because they were distributing pamphlets that they had anything to do with the Watts riots."

Younger also noted that "some communists and extremists claim credit for starting certain of the recent riots, but they are just bragging. The fact is that all the recent riots have started accidentally, triggered by some explainable incident."

The President's National Advisory Commission on Civil Disorders examined disturbances that erupted in 23 cities across the nation during the summer of 1967.

The commission's report concluded that the disorders "were not caused by, nor were they the consequence of, any organized plan or conspiracy. Specifically, the commission has found no evidence that all or any of the disorders or the incidents that led to them were planned or directed by any organization or group, international, national or local."

But then the report added, "Militant organizations, local and national, and individual agitators, who repeatedly forecast and called for violence, were active in the spring and summer of 1967. We believe that they deliberately sought to encourage violence, and that they did have an effect in creating an atmosphere that contributed to the outbreak of disorder."

There is ample evidence of activity by communists and other extremists before, during, and after riots. It is not surprising that communists should jump in whenever social unrest is ripe for exploding into violence. Though they pay lip service to peaceful, constitutional procedures, this is purely a tactical move to reduce the pressure of the police and the courts. In their hearts, they know they cannot come to power by peaceful, constitutional means. They always have been taught, and they believe, that the only road is by violence—and that is the one they embark upon whenever they feel they can do so with relative impunity.

Chapter Five

Guerrilla Tactics

Extremists of the American left, studying the guerrilla tactics employed so successfully in Cuba, Algeria, and Vietnam, are tailoring them for use in the United States. Guerrilla warfare is the tactic being taken up by those leftists who look to Mao, Castro, Che Guevara, and Ho Chi Minh for inspiration. Their aim is to destroy the ability of the government to maintain order and eventually to overthrow the government itself.

American advocates of guerrilla warfare talk about "urban" guerrilla warfare, as distinct from the predominantly rural type developed by their mentors in China, Cuba, and Vietnam. It would be geared to exploiting the special conditions of a highly mechanized and computerized society, which is vulnerable to complete blackout at the touch of a button or the blowing of a fuse. Sabotage would be the instrument used to paralyze our electric power and mechanized equipment. Terrorism would be used to immobilize urban dwellers, to make cities uninhabitable, and to close down offices and plants.

Could guerrilla warfare actually get under way in the United States? Is it anything more than just wild talk by wild people? Who are the men advocating it?

Guerrilla warfare is a common topic among members of SDS,

Who's Who on the Far Left
Republic of New Africa (RNA)

Position: Advocates establishing black nation within U.S. borders, consisting of all of South Carolina, Georgia, Alabama, Mississippi, and Louisiana. Follows Mao Tse-tung brand of revolutionary Marxism.

Leadership; Robert F. Williams, president; Milton R. and Richard Henry; Herman Ferguson; Joan Franklin; LeRoi Jones; Ron Karenga; Betty Shabazz (widow of Malcolm X).

Location: Headquarters, Detroit, Michigan. "Consulates" in several major cities.

Character: All-black, violently antiwhite adult movement, largely drawn from the ranks of Malcolm X's admirers. Malcolm X advocated armed violence and separatism and invented the slogan "by any means necessary" for his objectives before his death in 1965.

Brief History: The "nation" was founded in March 1968 at the Shrine of the Black Madonna (Central United Church of Christ, Detroit, Michigan). About 190 signed a declaration of independence declaring all blacks "forever free and independent of the jurisdiction of the United States." Robert F. Williams, then in exile in Peking to avoid arrest on kidnapping charges, was named president; H. Rap Brown was later named minister of defense.

On March 30, 1969, at the second national convention in Detroit, one police officer was shot and others were wounded during a skirmish after a conference. The arrest of some BPP members in New York City a few days later included 4 who had also been arrested in Detroit.

In May 1969 the State Department was officially informed by Brother Imari (Richard Henry) that $200 billion in "damages" was due New Africa, in addition to their southern territory. That amount has now been doubled.

the Black Panthers, the Progressive Labor Party, and the Republic of New Africa. The Communist Party-U.S.A. disavows any interest in such violent tactics. Its leaders continue to claim that they are advocating change through constitutional means.

But the New Left does not shy away from violence. Talk of guerrilla warfare started when rioting erupted in Negro slums in major American cities. Now it is discussed as a tactic to replace full-scale rioting. The intensity of rioting started to decline in the summer of 1968 and continued to do so in 1969. The riots no longer appear to be a potential first step in a Marxist revolution.

It is belived that extremists played a small role, if any, in starting the riots. But once the violence started, they worked hard at keeping it going. Nevertheless, official studies show that their ability to control events was limited.

They sought a new tactic which could be controlled more easily. The answer, said extremists such as Robert F. Williams of RAM, was guerrilla warfare, well-planned attacks on specific targets.

Guerrilla warfare as practiced in Cuba and Vietnam would not work in the United States, said Williams, pointing out that—

> the old method of guerrilla warfare, as carried out from the hills and countryside, would be ineffective in a powerful country like the U.S.A. Any such force would be wiped out in an hour. . . . The new concept calls for lightning campaigns conducted in highly sensitive urban communities, with the paralysis reaching the small communities and spreading to the farm areas. . . . The new concept is to huddle as close to the enemy as possible so as to neutralize his modern and fierce weapons.

And from Stokely Carmichael came this statement: "More people are now beginning to plan seriously a major urban guerrilla warfare . . . where we can move seriously within this country to bring it to its knees."

Sanger describes the events from peaceful protest to violence:

> Peaceful demonstrations lead to nuisance demonstrations, which lead to scattered violence. If that doesn't bring results,

Who's Who on the Far Left

Student National Coordinating Committee (SNCC)

Position: Supports international "black" revolution.

Leadership: James Forman, director of international affairs; H. Rap Brown; Philip Hutchings.

Location: Headquarters, Atlanta, Georgia.

Character: Young black adult revolutionaries; antiwhite; membership of about 200 active political organizers.

Brief History: Founded as Student Nonviolent Coordinating Committee in October 1960 by Martin Luther King as integrated, civil rights group. Dedicated northern revolutionaries from groups like PLP began work, winter 1961, to radicalize SNCC. Summer 1964, SNCC and its supporters sustained at least 1,000 arrests, 35 shooting incidents, 8 beatings, 6 murders in Mississippi work. Children of known Communists have become SNCC volunteers. In 1965, SNCC abandoned nonviolent teachings of Gandhi and King for those of Malcolm X ("by any means necessary") and Frantz Fanon (The Wretched of the Earth: all "white" systems are inherently evil). Ideal of integration abandoned for that of Black Power. Carmichael said in 1966: "When you talk of black power, you talk of bringing the country to its knees. When you talk of black power, you talk of building a movement that will smash everything Western civilization has created." As of 1966, no white members were allowed. SNCC is aligned with black groups which advocate revolution. In 1967, Brown succeeded Carmichael as national secretary. In 1968, Hutchings, new national director, started "black unity" efforts with groups such as CORE, ACTION, Zulu 1200s, and Black Liberators. February 17, 1968, SNCC and BPP merged. Forman, Brown, and Carmichael became BPP officers. July 1968, Forman and Brown "allegedly" resigned from BPP. "Nonviolent" was officially dropped from the name. April 26, 1969, Forman delivered "Black Manifesto" for National Black Economic Development Conference demanding $500 million from white churches for past "exploitation" of Negroes.

the next step usually takes the form of underground activities—
material terror, the smashing of windows, the burning of cars,
and a more widespread use of the sort of thing we have already
seen in a limited way in some of our cities.

After that comes explosive terror, where picked and trained
elements in the mobs begin to use guns and bombs. Personal
terror and assassination fit into this stage. . . . Finally, this all
builds up to general terror—the sort of violence that was so
messy and effective in Algeria—rebels putting bombs in suit-
cases and leaving them in streetcars, movie theaters or on
airplanes.

Are there any signs of organized guerrilla warfare activity in
the United States? Here are some cited by the FBI:

• Within a five-day period in September 1968, three ROTC
establishments were sabotaged.

• On September 29, 1968, the local CIA office at Ann Arbor,
Michigan, home of the University of Michigan, was bombed.
More than 10 individuals identified with New Left organizations
have been charged with that bombing as well as the bombings
of a Selective Service office at Roseville, Michigan, an Army
vehicle at Detroit, and the Science and Technology Building at
the University of Michigan.

• Five persons active in New Left groups have been charged
with a series of bombings in the San Francisco area, including the
destruction of three Pacific Gas and Electric Company towers.

• Michael Siskind, a student at Washington University in St.
Louis and a member of SDS, pleaded guilty February 20, 1969,
to charges stemming from the attempted firebombing of the
ROTC headquarters on campus. He was sentenced to five years
in prison.

• A federal grand jury in Denver indicted Cameron David Bishop, described by the FBI as an SDS activist, in connection with
the dynamiting of power transmission towers in the Denver area.

Incidents such as these follow a pattern advocated in a pamphlet prepared in Toronto, Canada, and distributed among many
New Left groups, particularly SDS. Titled "What Must We Do

Who's Who on the Far Left
Revolutionary Action Movement (RAM)

Position: Advocates international "black" revolution; identifies itself with ideology of Mao Tse-tung; endorses Cuban and North African guerrilla warriors.

Leadership: Robert F. Williams, president; Maxwell Stanford, head of U.S. operations.

Location: Headquarters, New York City, Philadelphia, Peking. About 200 hard-core members.

Character: Highly secret, black, violently antiwhite adult group; leadership interlocks with RNA.

Brief History: August 1961, Williams, who had armed his followers as leader of the Monroe, North Carolina, NAACP, fled to Cuba to avoid arrest on kidnapping charges. RAM was organized in winter 1963, with Williams as leader-in-exile. It began to set up front organizations, such as Black Brotherhood Improvement Association, Black Liberation Front (1964), Jamaica Rifle and Pistol Club, Black Panther Party in N.Y.C. (August 1966), and Black Arts Repertory Theater, led by LeRoi Jones. In 1964, guerrilla activity began in Harlem. August 1966, Stanford said: "Black men must unite in overthrowing their white oppressors, stalking by night and sparing no one." May 1967 the "Black Guard" was set up in New York City to operate under the dictatorship of a secret "soul circle." 1967, Herman Ferguson, minister of education (now minister of defense for RNA), was convicted for his part in a conspiracy to murder civil rights leaders Roy Wilkins and Whitney Young.

Major RAM manifesto, "World Black Revolution," outlines 3-stage operation: (1) education and recruitment; (2) obtaining funds both legally and illegally; (3) direct action, implemented by use of teenage groups in larger cities. Late 1967, activities went underground. In 1969, Williams returned from his 8-year Cuba-Peking exile. Jones leads "black arts" movement in Newark to give ghetto youths "psychological arsenal" of pride and dedication to black nationalism.

Now," the pamphlet was an argument in favor of sabotage to be directed primarily at Selective Service offices and induction centers.

"Is there anyone who doubts," says the pamphlet, "that a small homemade incendiary device with a timing mechanism planted in a broom closet at the Oakland induction center could result in fire and smoke damage to the entire building thus making it unusable for weeks or months?"

As for draft boards, the pamphlet recommends that "in small towns where many draft boards are relatively old frame structures and where police patrols are spotty, simple Molotov cocktails can be thrown through windows from side streets. . . .

An example of the work of extreme left-wing operators: results of a bomb which blasted the fourth and fifth floors of the Army induction center at 39 Whitehall Street, New York City, knocking out two walls and shattering more than 40 windows.

Who's Who on the Far Left

Black Panther Party (BPP)

Position: Advocates guerrilla warfare as taught by Mao Tse-tung and Che Guevara for achieving revolution in the United States.

Leadership: Huey P. Newton, Bobby George Seale, Eldridge Cleaver, Kathleen Cleaver, Franklyn Jones, David Hilliard, Donald L. Cox, Stokely Carmichael, George Mason Murray, Ivanhoe Donaldson.

Location: Headquarters, Oakland, California; estimated 4,000 hard-core members in 26 branch offices.

Character: Young black revolutionary activists. August 18, 1968, Newton stated: "We consider ourselves as an integral part of the army of resistance that is being mobilized all over the world."

Brief History: Courtland Cox, classmate of Carmichael at Howard University, invented the name "Black Panther Party" for SNCC's political arm in Alabama in 1965. Maxwell Stanford (RAM) founded a BPP of young, armed guerrillas in New York City, August 1966. October 1966, Newton and Seale founded the Oakland group which became headquarters. After Newton was convicted for shooting a policeman, BPP set up "Free Huey" as a rallying cry and called him today's major "political prisoner." July 1968, "red book" of Chairman Mao and "black book" of Nkrumah became required reading. October 1968, BPP headquarters was also headquarters of the Black Student Union; Senate testimony indicates that many black student groups have interlocking membership with the BPP. Since Cox visited Mobile, Alabama, to instruct Negro youths in making and using fire- and acid bombs, the city has had 126 arson cases, over 50 blamed on these devices. February 1969, BPP began a program to feed an estimated 34,000 children breakfast and politics. Merchants are terrified into contributing; appeal to ghetto residents is that of Robin Hood's Merry Band. According to an ex-Panther, the cream of the BPP is the "Black Guard," which must "commit any act of violence that the Party directs."

Furthermore, simply continually breaking windows and strewing parking lots with broken glass and bent carpet tacks are relatively minor but effective methods of harassing Selective Service employes."

The pamphlet goes on to describe the sort of people who would be most effective in carrying out this type of antiwar activity: "They will most likely be (if they are to be successful) highly motivated, meticulously calculating and thoroughly dedicated. . . . They will be ordinary students, professors, community workers, nine-to-five office workers, teachers, etc., who lead normal lives and carry normal public and private relationships, but who (perhaps at intervals of 3 to 5 months) will destroy property of Selective Service."

Like so much of this new literature of guerrilla warfare circulating among the left, the pamphlet concludes with drawings and instructions on the preparation of time bombs and Molotov cocktails.

Within groups like SDS, the emphasis continues to be on a guerrilla warfare waged against property. It is regarded as a tactic to disrupt what SDS calls the "war machine." The instructions in pamphlets such as the one cited above recommend firebombing installations in early morning hours when they would be empty and there would be no chance of injuring employees. There are other groups of the New Left who are little concerned about possible injury to people.

Black extremist groups such as the Black Panthers, RAM, and the recently formed Republic of New Africa advocate using guerrilla warfare tactics against authorities, particularly police.

The best known of the Panthers, Eldridge Cleaver, fled to Cuba and then to Algeria to avoid having to return to a California prison on charges stemming from a gun battle with Oakland police. Cleaver, whose title is minister of information of the Panthers, has led the all-black organization farther and farther to the left.

Panther members study the writings of Mao Tse-tung. They also receive extensive training in guerrilla warfare tactics. The FBI reports that Panther members receive instructions on making

Huey Newton, right, defense minister and top-ranking official of the Black Panther Party, is now serving a prison sentence of 2 to 15 years for voluntary manslaughter in the shooting of a police officer. With him is Bobby Seale, the Party's national chairman.

and using Molotov cocktails. It also reports that the party is establishing guerrilla warfare schools in California.

Two former Panthers, Jean and Larry Powell, told a Congressional committee that the party apparently has adopted an old communist technique of political robberies. One of the pioneers of this tactic in prerevolutionary Russia was Stalin. Powell was arrested late in 1968 for an armed robbery that he said was carried out on orders from the Black Panther Party. According to Powell, such activities bring $50,000 to $100,000 a month into the party's national headquarters in Oakland, California.

Bank robbery is a simple type of political robbery. Stores are also broken into for such items as radios, guns, and liquor.

Larry Clayton Powell, 25, and his wife Jean, 24, tell a Senate investigation subcommittee in Washington of their experiences in the Black Panther Party, including assassinations, beatings, and armed robberies by squads assigned to raise money for the organization.

Robert F. Williams, while in Communist China, counseled his followers in RAM and the Republic of New Africa in techniques of guerrilla warfare. The following are typical examples of the advice given in his pamphlet the *Crusader:*

> Plans should be made ahead of time by groups of less than 10 people to have certain targets in mind (such as police stations and other utilities used to suppress the rebellion). These should be destroyed. . . .
>
> Since we are fighting guerrilla warfare, the guerrillas must station themselves so that they can catch the troops in a crossfire while giving each other protection. . . .
>
> If you are tired of being shot at by the police, open your door for a fighting brother to use your window to kill a honky cop. . . .
>
> Anytime something involves the life and death of a guerrilla, he has the right to force at gunpoint any "so-called Negro" who refuses to cooperate, but the guerrilla, on the other hand, must never take advantage of his people, for when he does he takes on the characteristics of the enemy and must be treated as such (an enemy to the black revolution).

The long-range target of these extremist groups is American society. The immediate target is the police. It is the police who often are singled out for some of the most extreme tactics advocated by these groups.

An example is a mimeographed pamphlet circulated among striking students at San Francisco State College. Called *Your Manual,* the pamphlet described a number of makeshift weapons.

Rocks and bottles were said to be "very effective if thrown by numbers of rebels. An empty bottle or rock can disable a pig for the whole campaign." Recommended for use against mounted policemen were red pepper, darts, water guns filled with household ammonia, ice picks, sling shots, and cherry bombs to which tacks had been glued.

What is the effect of the antipolice, anti-authority tracts circulated by the extremists of the left? The most dangerous result has

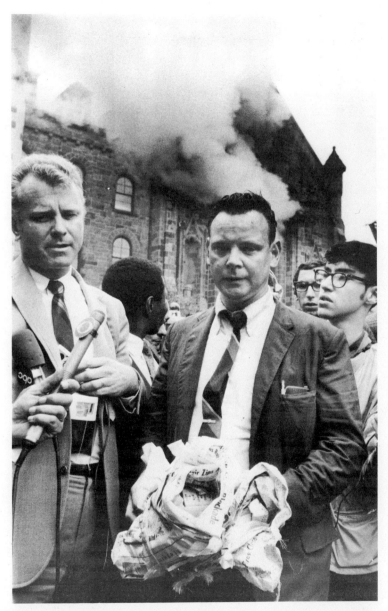

Patrick Crowley, New York City fire marshal, displays a fire bomb similar to one believed to have caused the blaze seen burning in the background at the Finley Student Center on the City College of New York campus. Fires broke out on the campus following five violent skirmishes between police and radical students.

Black extremist leader Fred Ahmed Evans (center), heavily chained and flanked by police officers, is taken to Ohio State Penitentiary after being convicted on seven charges of first degree murder at Cleveland.

been greatly to increase tensions between police and black extremist groups. There has been an increase in shooting incidents, often resulting in the killing and wounding of individuals involved.

An example of this could be seen in the events at Cleveland the night of July 23, 1968. The incident involved police and a black extremist group called the Black Nationalists of New Libya headed by Fred Ahmed Evans. The gunfight between Evans's heavily armed followers and the police left four black civilians and three white policemen dead. Evans later was convicted of murder.

A report on the incident submitted to the National Commission on the Causes and Prevention of Violence notes that it was never determined who shot first.

The report concluded that—

> the violence that erupted in Cleveland at the end of July, 1968, may have marked the beginning of a new pattern. . . . It began as violence, aimed at personal injury. . . . A small well-equipped army of black extremists were responsible for the bloodshed (whether or not they fired the first shot). The depths of anger and extreme beliefs from which the violence sprung are indicated by the fact that the presence of a Negro in the mayor's chair [Mayor Carl B. Stokes] did not prevent it from happening.

Leftist groups such as the Student Nonviolent Coordinating Committee quickly labeled the incident "the first stage of revolutionary armed struggle." But Mayor Stokes described the incident as "spontaneous action taken by a group who were armed and emotionally prepared to do violence." A Cuyahoga County grand jury agreed with Stokes's assessment.

Those who advocate maintaining the sort of tension between police and extremist groups as existed in Cleveland can find support for their view in Marx. He wrote that "while the democratic petty bourgeoisie would like to bring the revolution to a close as soon as their demands are more or less complied with, it is in our interest and our taste to make the revolution permanent, to keep it going until all the ruling and possessing classes are deprived of power."

But it is Che Guevara and Fidel Castro, architects of the Cuban communist revolution, who get the most attention from guerrilla warfare advocates in the United States. For they are the men who made the tactic work in the Western Hemisphere.

As Guevara wrote in his book, *Guerrilla Warfare,* one of the major contributions of the Cuban revolution was its demonstration that "people's forces can win a war against the army." Guevara's writings on guerrilla warfare are read avidly by extremists who hope to adapt his methods to the highly urbanized conditions in the United States.

Carmichael, Cleaver, and various leaders of SDS all have made pilgrimages to Cuba. Some, like Cleaver, left disillusioned to proceed to another center of guerrilla warfare training, Algeria.

But others stay on in Cuba. J. Edgar Hoover told a congressional committee: "Information has come to our attention that Negroes are being trained in Cuba for infiltration into the United States. This is particularly important when viewed in the light of open support given during several recent international communist conferences held in Havana to the concept of armed insurrection by black power advocates and other black extremist groups in the United States."

However, for a guerrilla movement to succeed it must have the support of the people. And here lies the weakness of the guerrilla tactic in the United States. Its practitioners have not yet been able to develop the sort of mass following needed to help them to escape apprehension after a violent assault on authority.

Chapter Six

Target: Youth

In the 1930s, with the nation nearly knocked out by the blows of the stock market crash and the great depression, communists saw an opportunity to invade both the universities and the trade unions. In the eyes of Moscow and its American followers in the United States, students and workers could be the two elements for producing a communist revolution. Students potentially were the fuse for touching off an explosion—an uprising—by the workers.

The communists scored notable successes in both areas. In a relatively short period of time, they converted some of the most brilliant students to Marxism. Many subsequently were disillusioned, and communist influence on the campus waned as the depression faded away, the United States was swept into World War II, and Stalin discredited the Soviet Union by his pact with Hitler.

The 1960s produced a new situation and a new opportunity for communists to invade the campuses of the United States. The opportunity was created by the three major elements previously mentioned:

1. Rising sentiment against the Vietnam war, due in no small measure to young men who simply did not care to run the risk of losing their lives in a war in Vietnam or anywhere else.

2. Widespread sympathy among white students and increasing militancy among black students in support of civil rights and a better deal for the black population.

3. Growing resentment against the university "establishment," accused of being insensitive to the needs of a new generation and of contributing to creation of a sterilized, mechanized, and refrigerated life in the United States.

These three elements combined to produce violence on campuses and in cities throughout the country. And, among other things, they had the effect of blowing open the doors to a revival of Marxist philosophy and an invasion of communist operators on college and university campuses.

To professional communists, the new opportunities were breathtaking. For the first time in more than 30 years, they saw a chance not only to establish new cells but actually to win over some of the major campuses of the country to the Marxist cause.

And the potential now was even greater than it was in the 1930s because American university students had become greater in number, more politically developed, and more disposed to action, including violence.

The number of U.S. college students now approaches 7 million. They outnumber the armed forces 2 to 1. Whereas only 2 percent of our young population went to college a century ago, about 40 percent are on the campus today.

Furthermore, there are three times as many students in the nation's 26,000 public secondary schools as there are in the 1,600 four-year public and private colleges and universities. And the high schools, too, have attracted the active interest of communists and Marxists.

In short, the youth of the United States are a prime target of extremist elements who hope to use them for achieving their political aims. Communists and Marxists calculate that if they can capture the minds of American youth, they will capture the future of the nation.

Their immediate job is to do the hard missionary work of getting Marxist principles out of the books and into the heads of the students. It is also to provide the excitement of action which comes from mass meetings, protest demonstrations, and violence against established authority. Clashes with police, as noted, help to discredit the "establishment," of which the police are the symbol and the representative, and to inflame the bitter passions of young people.

Communists and Marxists already have been notably successful with their indoctrination work. They have made Marxism respectable on the U.S. campus. It is no longer a dirty word.

The fact that there is something of a "babel" of Marxism on the U.S. campus today does not detract from the achievement. Professor Philip G. Altbach of the University of Wisconsin, an authority on the radical student movement, says that "various political tendencies co-exist within SDS, from Maoism and radical Marxism to anarchism and democratic socialism."

The point to be observed, however, is that Marxism runs through all these different tendencies and provides something which is common to them all, just as the red flag is common to leftist movements of different shades. The fact is that each student who goes over to the Marxist side, whatever its complexion, can be chalked up by the communists, by the Russians, and by the Red Chinese as a gain for them and a loss for the capitalist structure in the United States.

The New Left on the U.S. campus may be said to be as deeply divided as the communist world outside the United States. Racial and political differences have produced these three major factions:

• Regulars. This faction of the SDS advocates a loose coalition of young people, the poor, and the racial minorities for the purpose of bringing about revolutionary change in the structure of American society. Undisciplined, often to the point of anarchy, the regulars nevertheless managed to carry the SDS to the forefront of New Left youth movements.

• Progessive Labor. This group attempted to take over leadership of SDS at its 1969 convention. Highly disciplined, they are dedicated to the doctrines of Mao Tse-tung and are known as "hard-line" Marxists, as distinguished from the "soft line" taken by many Regulars.

• Black students. Increasingly, these students have been moving

Members of SDS at the University of Connecticut, after occupying the school's administration building and forcing cancellation of campus recruiting by Dow Chemical Company because it manufactured napalm for use in the Vietnam war.

away from alliances with the predominantly white SDS. In part, this is due to a desire for an all-black organization, an inverted form of segregation developing from "black nationalism" and "black power" extremism of the Black Panther type.

The effect of the split between the Regulars and the Progressive Labor Maoists may be to make both factions even more militant as they compete for the support of fellow radicals. Marxists looking on from the outside, say from Moscow, Peking, and Hanoi, could hardly be displeased by such developments.

The Regulars announced that they would escalate their antiwar activities, and they indicated what they had in mind by electing Mark Rudd as national secretary of SDS. Rudd gained fame as leader of the demonstrations that paralyzed Columbia University.

During five days of rioting at Columbia in the spring of 1968, extremists seized five university buildings, occupied the offices of Grayson Kirk, who subsequently resigned as president of the university, and held the dean of the college prisoner for 24 hours.

The significance of the Columbia rioting was described as follows by Tom Hayden, one of the founders of SDS:

> Columbia opened a new tactical stage in the resistance movement which began last fall: from the overnight occupation of buildings to permanent occupation; from mill-ins to the creation of revolutionary committees; from symbolic civil disobedience to barricaded resistance. Not only are these tactics already being duplicated on other campuses, but they are sure to be surpassed by even more militant tactics.

Mark Rudd, in the heat of his "victory" at Columbia, made it clear that his aim was to promote a Marxist revolution. He directed these words to the "defeated" President Kirk:

> You are quite right in feeling that the situation is "potentially dangerous." For if we win, we will take control of your world, your corporation, your university and attempt to mold a world in which we and other people can live as human beings. Your power is directly threatened, since we will have to destroy that power before we take over. We begin by fight-

ing you about your support of the war in Vietnam and American imperialism—IDA [Institute of Defense Analysis] and the School for International Affairs. We will fight you about your control of black people in Morningside Heights, Harlem, and the campus itself. And we will fight you about the type of miseducation you are trying to channel us through. We will have to destroy at times, even violently, in order to end your power and your system—but this is a far cry from nihilism. . . . We, the young people, whom you so rightly fear, say that the society is sick and you and your capitalism are the sickness. You call for order and respect for authority; we call for

Mark Rudd, leader of the 1968 campus revolt at Columbia University (which later won him the leadership of SDS), uses a bullhorn to address incoming freshmen at Columbia.

justice, freedom and socialism. There is only one thing left to
say. It may sound nihilistic to you, since it is the opening shot
in a war of liberation. I'll use the words of LeRoi Jones, whom
I'm sure you don't like a whole lot: "Up against the wall,
———— ————, this is a stick up."

There undoubtedly are differences between the white Maoists
and the white Regulars, but the words and actions of Mark Rudd,
as a leader of the Regulars, make the differences difficult to see.
They appear to arise over a struggle for power between different
groups of SDS and the New Left, rather than over doctrines of
Marxism, on which they essentially are in agreement.

Both friends and foes express the view that the New Left eventually may destroy itself as a result of fratricidal feuding among its
members. The different factions often attack each other as violently
as they assault "the common enemy—imperialism and the establishment." An example of how rival groups treat one another can
be found in this report published in the July 8, 1969, issue of
New Left Notes, the SDS newspaper:

At Queens College, Berkeley, and many other places, in
struggles against the ruling class, Progressive Labor has worked
to defuse and constrict actions with their definite non-struggle
views on tactics. They have come down against examining files
and building barricades because they think that such actions
would be construed as destruction of private property and
hence would alienate people.

In an unprecedented pig move 75 PL and WSA[Worker-Student
Alliance] people attacked the New York SDS regional assembly
at New York University's Eisner-Lubin Auditorium Monday
night. While 150 SDS people were meeting the group ran
through the lobby ripping up furniture and charged the door-
way leading to the Auditorium. In their attempt to gain access
to the meeting they smashed a plate-glass wall with furniture
parts and ash cans.

The meeting continued inside in a disciplined fashion. A
small security force kept the outsiders from entering and dis-

rupting it. Fire hoses were used to keep them in the lobby. Several of our people were hurt, not only by flying glass but by direct blows and clubbings with chair and table legs. Five people were taken to a hospital emergency room.

In practice PL has consistently cooled people from militant actions which threaten the ruling class. It is clear that this action was designed 1) to create a situation in which the cops would be called in and people would be busted, 2) to make it impossible for the SDS chapter at NYU to gain access to University facilities in the future, and 3) to purposely injure people. Cops did come and clear the lobby; that no one was busted at that time was due to the discipline of the SDS people, in the meeting and on the security force.

Now that SDS has acted against PL's counter-revolutionary politics by kicking them out of the organization, we can expect them to become even more vicious and unprincipled. Attacking a meeting in this fashion is pig work. We should learn from the example of our brothers and sisters in New York and exercise discipline in these situations. Our politics will win the struggle.

Black students may be less concerned with overthrowing the capitalist system than they are with the more immediate problem of getting a "bigger piece" of the university. This would take the form of more places, more rights, and more privileges for black students.

Nevertheless, under the influence of such off-campus extremist groups as the Black Panthers, the Maoist brand of Marxism is reported to have taken hold and to be spreading among black students. It is difficult to find, among either white or black students, any impressive exponent of a doctrine or philosophy which would counter the appeal being made by Marxism.

There are, however, some things which might blunt campus discontent which the Marxists exploit. Robert Finch, secretary of health, education, and welfare, acknowledges that "there are some hard-core militants in the SDS who think they can contest, challenge, overthrow these institutions as we know them." He adds: "The basic problem goes to the higher educational institution, its rigidity and its unwillingness to respond to the demands of the community around it and the students."

As students became frustrated with their seeming inability to "get through" to their elders, their tactics became more extreme. In 1964, students at the University of California at Berkeley protested against a university ban prohibiting on-campus political activity. The protest developed into a massive confrontation between students and the administration. Eventually the university was paralyzed. Berkeley made students aware of their potential power, and students applied this lesson to campuses across the country, all the way to Columbia, on the East coast.

In the face of student tactics of "confrontation," involving

During a rally protesting ROTC at Tulane University in New Orleans, one man becomes the object of a tug of war between fellow demonstrators and the police.

violence, how are university administrations to respond? Morris Abram, president of Brandeis University, sees three choices:

> 1. The university can surrender to every whim to avoid confrontation—but if it does, it will not long be a place of excellence or, indeed, an institution of learning.
> 2. The university can resist by using outside force—which probably would result in its becoming both bitter and divided.
> 3. The university can attempt to set agreed limits as a community, and try internally to enforce this code. Such rules must originate primarily with the students and faculties. They must be a statement of necessities as seen by the persons to be governed, and they will, it is hoped, have an internal validity which makes them almost self-enforcing.

Abram has had some success by applying the third choice and providing the kind of response suggested by Secretary Finch.

Other schools, however, took the second choice, with the outcome indicated by Abram. The consequences of calling in police to settle the issue at Columbia University were described as follows by Daniel Bell, professor of sociology:

> In all, about a hundred students were hurt. But it was not the violence itself that was so horrible. Despite the many pictures in the papers of bleeding students, not one required hospitalization. It was the capriciousness of that final action. The police simply ran wild. Those who tried to say they were innocent bystanders or faculty were given the same flailing treatment as the students. For most of the students it was their first encounter with brutality and blood, and they responded in fear and anger. The next day almost the entire campus responded to a call for a student strike. In a few hours, thanks to the New York City Police Department, a large part of the Columbia campus had become radicalized.

University presidents, while trying to avoid the use of outside force, are nevertheless subject to acute provocation by extremists of all Marxist groups. As student leadership becomes increasingly radical, the thrust of campus activity shifts from satisfaction of student needs to fulfillment of communist political objectives.

Thus, Marxist extremists are rioting on campuses not to get more rights for students but to get more students for communist and Marxist movements.

They are interested in civil rights not to help the black man but to help the communists multiply their numbers so they will be able to produce a revolution.

And they are interested in peace movements not so much to end the war in Vietnam as to strengthen communism in the United States.

In short, any riot, any protest, and any demonstration—whether for sex, miniskirts, hot air, or cold air—is worthy of support by

Antidraft demonstrators indulge themselves at the fountain pool of San Francisco City Hall during a "peace demonstration."

the Old Left and the New Left so long as the net result serves the communist objectives: to alienate students from the "establishment," radicalize them with Marxist dogma, and then throw them into the "war against capitalism."

Attorney General John Mitchell observed: "This has gone beyond the pale of a student demonstration. These are acts of militants who are entering upon a conspiracy."

U.S. government agents have noticed that many of the militant organizers going from campus to campus stirring up trouble are "nonstudents." It would not be surprising if a good number of these nonstudents also happened to be members of the Communist Party.

Attracted by the new opportunities on the U.S. campus, the National Executive Committee of the Communist Party met in New York City in August 1960 to consider a face-lifting operation which would enhance its appeal to American youth.

Daniel Rubin, the party's national youth director, proposed the formation of a popular front group—a familiar communist tactic—this one aimed at young people.

Rubin was sent on a tour of college campuses to see how much support there was for a left-wing youth group. The results were surprising. Rubin found few American college students ready to join the Communist Party ranks, but he discovered an intense curiosity about the American communist view of the world. He began receiving invitations to address campus audiences.

Soon, invitations were rolling in to other party leaders. Dr. Herbert Aptheker became a familiar figure on the campus lecture circuit. So did other prominent communists, including Elizabeth Gurley Flynn, Benjamin J. Davis, Jr., Carl Winter, James Jackson, and Hyman Lumer.

Encouraged by the reception they received, the communists intensified their efforts. They began actively seeking speaking engagements. Arnold Johnson, party information director, sent letters to college newspaper editors and student councils, saying:

> May we request you to invite representatives of the Communist Party to speak at forums of the student body of your

Herbert Aptheker, prominent leader of the Communist Party in the United States, addresses about 500 students at the University of Wisconsin after U.S. campuses, under pressure by the New Left, reopen their doors to spokesmen of the Old Left. These students gave Aptheker a standing ovation after he called for a halt to the Vietnam war.

school either in the form of lectures, by participation in symposia or in debates?

...Students in their search for knowledge apparently desire a fair exchange of opinion on the supreme problems facing our country, with all viewpoints represented and they reject the widespread practice of denouncing communism without affording the communists a chance to be heard. . . .

Arrangements for communist speakers can be made by addressing the lecture and information bureau. Where colleges or student groups are in a position to do so we would appreciate the usual fee and expenses paid other speakers. Where schools or groups are financially not in a position to cover the expenses involved, we shall try to do so to the best of our ability.

Since they launched the speaking program, party leaders have made nearly 400 campus appearances. During each of the past few school years, they have spoken at more than 50 different institutions.

"I get a reception on campuses that I never got before," said Hall. "Three, four, five years ago, communist speakers were banned on most college and university campuses. Today, I have so many invitations that I have to turn most of them down."

Hall also said that "the struggle to hear the communist viewpoint from the communists became an important part of the popular mass upsurge. It is to the everlasting credit of the young generation that they broke down the walls of silence.... It was these young Americans who spearheaded the fight to get Marxism and the viewpoint of the Communist Party into the marketplace of ideas. . . . Our concept of speaking to the millions became a reality."

To J. Edgar Hoover, the party's lecture program represents a serious threat:

> Among other things, the party hopes to capitalize on the radicalism of the so-called New Left movement. The basic purpose, however, behind the speaking program, which has been pursued with vigor since the early 1960s, is to gain recognition for and acceptance of the Communist Party-U.S.A. as a legitimate political party on the American scene. The party considers that college campuses offer an excellent opportunity to reach the youth who will be the leaders of tomorrow.

The FBI director notes that "at first, party speakers tried, basically, to arouse student and faculty interest in the party and communism. But soon, as Aptheker reported, party leaders found their campus receptions cordial and friendly. In due course, they were making speeches about current international and national events, about history, philosophy, social conditions, even religion,

Campus demonstrations inspired by SDS spread to Harvard University in April 1969, as students stage a three-day strike in support of demands made by protesters.

giving the communist viewpoint."

What is the viewpoint communist speakers present to young Americans?

Using a telephone hookup, Hall addressed students at five Rocky Mountain schools—Arizona State, Colorado State, Utah State, and the Universities of Utah and Wyoming. None of the five is considered a hotbed of radicalism. Hall's message delivered these points:

> I am for reforms that are in the best interest of our working class and the American people and, more basically, I am for a revolutionary change in our economic and social system.

A demonstrator cavorts in the San Francisco Civic Center Plaza fountain during a peace march protesting the draft and the Vietnam war.

It is a hard reality of our time that one-third of mankind is in the process of building such a system. There are variations from country to country based on specific conditions in each country, but they all call the new system socialism, which is the present stage of the building of the future system of communism. No country has yet reached the stage of communism.

He assured his listeners that "our socialism will be a product of our experience as a people. It will be a response to our problems as a nation."

And he repeated the party's current peace-loving, coexistence line: "We, in common with most of the world's Marxists, are per-

Three members of the "Future Generation" picket outside a Hollywood Sunset Strip restaurant in protest against any interference by the "establishment" with their public disturbances.

suaded that war is no longer inevitable. . . . It strikes us as folly
to think that monopoly can be overcome and revolutionary transformation of society be undertaken without the sanction and
participation of a majority of the people. . . . We communists are
defenders of the Constitution in principle and practice."

Even religion, Marx's "opium of the people," gets a kind word:
"We recognize many positive, humanist values in the ethical and
moral precepts of the several religions."

In trying to make the Communist Party seem respectable, Hall
sometimes sounds only slightly to the left of the chamber of commerce. This, of course, makes the Moscow oriented communists
less appealing to campus radicals.

Furthermore, the orthodox Communist Party in the United
States is handicapped by its identity with the Soviet Union. Campus
extremists, both white and black, look on the Soviet Union as a
country which, after achieving its own revolution, is now intent
on conserving what it possesses and, like an aging, prosperous
man, is not inclined to take risks or make sacrifices to help other
states carry out a revolution.

That is why, they believe, the Soviet Union speaks of "coexistence" with capitalism and takes a cautious position on guerrilla
warfare (said to be one of the reasons why Che Guevara broke
with the Soviet Union).

Cuba and Red China, on the other hand, are regarded as younger
communist states, more disposed to run risks and to make sacrifices. These take the form of fierce opposition to the United States
and support for guerrilla operations in noncommunist countries.

But whether of the Moscow or Peking brand, the fact is that
Marxism is marching ahead on the U.S. campus today. Behind
and beneath all the noise and violence about peace, civil rights,
and student rights, Marxist ideology has established a strong base
on the campus. This poses a challenge which may remain long
after the war has ended in Vietnam and students have secured
many of their legitimate demands.

Chapter Seven

Target: Labor

Leaders of the extreme left, having enlisted a good number of college and university students, are looking beyond the American campus to still bigger game—"the working class." It is an article of faith with Marxists that the proletariat is the key to revolution and to overthrow of the capitalist system. Therefore, one of the cardinal objectives of communism and the New Left is to win over the workers.

This may sound like an absurd undertaking in the United States, but both the Old and the New Left have been encouraged by two things: (1) the demonstrated capacity of the left to create chaos on the campus and in the cities; (2) the student-worker uprising of May 1968 in France.

The uprising in France cracked the position of President Charles de Gaulle and contributed to his subsequent downfall. It made such a deep impression on American extremists that it serves as their blueprint for duplicating the uprising in the United States someday. It may be worthwhile to recall the outline of the blueprint.

It started with a protest demonstration by a small minority of students at the Sorbonne, the heart of the University of Paris. They demanded large-scale educational reforms, including the right to participate in running the university.

The demonstration quickly developed into rioting. Students overturned automobiles and used them as barricades for pitched battles with police. The violence continued for days, spreading through the streets of Paris and the principal cities of France.

After raising the black flag of anarchism and the red flag of communism, students called on the trade unions to join in a general strike against the government. More than half of the nation's 19 million workers are reported to have responded.

The strike paralyzed the country. Subways, buses, and railroads shut down. So did banks, the Stock Exchange, department stores, and many food stores. The strike spread to oil refineries and numerous industries. Workers occupied a number of factories, mines, and shipyards. They often replaced the French tricolor with the red flag of rebellion.

President de Gaulle sought to make peace with his people, and he did manage to hold on for a time. But his prestige had been shattered by an uprising which had been triggered by a handful of radical students. His subsequent fall was hailed as a victory for those who had gone out on strike against him and his government.

The annual convention of the Students for a Democratic Society, flying the black and red flags of anarchism and communism, opened on June 9, 1968, at East Lansing, Michigan, in the wake of the student-worker uprising in France and of the rebellion at Columbia University in New York.

Reporting the proceedings, *Guardian*, the SDS paper, said both events had "a profound effect" on SDS members. The Paris uprising, according to the paper, demonstrated "the strength of the working class while at the same time pointing up the need for a revolutionary vanguard [of students]."

The Progressive Labor Party went all out for a "student-worker alliance" in the United States. Leaders of the SDS, while resisting PLP attempts to take over their group, agreed that such an alliance was necessary.

The SDS and other elements of the New Left, with the blessings of the Communist Party, accordingly embarked on a program which was intended to achieve two things:

1. Spread Marxism from the university campus to industrial areas

to radicalize the American proletariat.

2. Enable students to reach positions of close contact with American workers so that students someday might trigger a nationwide explosion comparable to or exceeding the one in France.

SDS, initiating action toward this end, proclaimed a "work-in." It called on students to do one or more of these three things:

1. Take a job in a factory during summer vacation and go to work on the employees.

Scene of student-worker uprising in Paris, 1968. U.S. students and workers are being urged by the far left to use it as a model to produce similar uprisings in this country.

2. Wherever there is a strike, join the workers in the picket line and thus develop close relationships.

3. Help organize blacks in their own labor unions.

SDS provided students with a manual which explained "how to research the job situation in your area," "what jobs to look for," "how to get a job," and "what to expect on the job."

Instructions on "jobs to look for" included the following:

Job-seekers should try to get hired in plants or transport depots that have several hundred (let's say a 400 minimum) workers. Reasons for this include: (a) If we want to reach workers with literature, the potential audience is greater; (b) the larger the company facility, the better chance that it will be in a basic union, that the workers will have some sense of organization (even if they think the union is a sellout one), and that therefore there will be a tie-in to workers nationally.

Within the larger plant situation, it might be desirable for students seeking jobs in the area or city in which their school is located to pick a place which would have follow-up possibilities in the Fall through contacts established within the plant, in line with an on-going worker-student alliance activity.

In general, people should seek unskilled jobs (probably couldn't get a skilled one anyway) and, if given the choice, a job where one would contact larger numbers of workers. If you are white, select a plant where the majority are white. . . . If black, a student would of necessity have to (and should) get a job where there are large numbers of black workers. Women should give special consideration to jobs where many women are employed. These include, in addition to basic industries (like electric) department stores, telephone companies, hospitals, and even some large offices which are unionized, etc.

In cases where people cannot travel to (or don't want to get jobs in) auto industries, large wholesale and retail outfits within the city proper could be as advantageous—large mail-order houses (Sears-Roebuck, Montgomery Ward department stores, preferably those with unions); possibly as non-professional workers in hospitals (although here in many large cities there are large majorities of black workers, a factor for white students to consider). Other such places could include the telephone company, mass utilities (if privately owned; government-owned usually requires a civil service test and waiting period).

Instructions on "how to get a job" include:

Some places hire students specifically for the summer as replacements for workers on vacations (although usually bosses try to get away with not filling in, unless the union contract has specific stipulations and they are enforced). Others won't hire you if they know you are a student or if they think you're only working for the summer. In MOST cases it would probably be best NOT to mention that you are a student. . . . If, then, it is the case of not being able to state you're a student seeking summer work, you have to come in as a job-seeker who has worked since graduating high-school (you should say you're a high school graduate), which means you have to have a place or person who will say you worked there for the past 1-4 years....

If you've been in [the armed forces] and had an honorable discharge, tell it the way it is. If you've had something other than an honorable discharge, avoid mentioning it; you've been "working since high school...."

Some places give aptitude tests. Don't show off. If you're taking the test with other job-seekers, try to see how far (number of questions) they're getting and adjust accordingly. If you do too well, they'll either be suspicious or want to use you in the "front office...."

You should be at your first place looking at around 8:30 or 9:00 A.M. It's hard to get a job if you start at 2:00 P.M. You generally should not wear a suit and tie or fancy dress, but DON'T dress like a slob. Slacks and sports shirt, with or without a sport jacket, depending on the weather, and skirt or summer dress with low heels (or at least not 6-inch spikes) for women.

If places require a "non-communist" or "non-subversive" signature, sign it....

Don't use $20 words. Don't put on a tough guy act. Just plain, simple language and attitude. Usually the less said, the better. Don't volunteer information. Just answer what is asked....

Do let [regularly employed workers] know you're a student fairly soon, within the first 2 or 3 weeks, as long as the foreman won't find out (or someone else who might use it to get you fired). But this isn't foolproof. You've got to play it by ear. But if you don't say you're a student, they'll know it and you won't be able to do an honest, straightforward job. Remember, although workers may think students are snobbish (and many are), they also respect education and want their kids to go to college. (That's why they're working so hard, among other reasons). Your job is to bring across the identity of interest of students and workers—the fact that without workers, there would be no universities, that the working class is the class with the power, that workers really create the value of society, that without them basic changes in the system can't happen, etc.

The "work-in" was first tried on a relatively small scale during the summer of 1968, with students taking factory jobs in Boston, Detroit, Chicago, and San Francisco. This was preliminary to launching the campaign during the summer of 1969 on a national scale, the country being divided into eight regions.

As vacation time approached, employers and trade unions were alerted to possible danger. Representative James M. Collins of Texas named 24 defense plants in the Southwest that he claimed had been selected as special SDS targets.

The New York Commerce and Industry Association sponsored a meeting, reported to have been attended by 250 businessmen, to discuss the alleged threat by SDS militants. Similar conferences were called in other cities across the country.

Arch N. Booth, executive vice president of the U.S. Chamber of Commerce, mailed warning letters to 3,800 businessmen, advising them to keep their "cool." He enclosed copies of the SDS "work-in" manual.

The Bell Aircraft Corporation at Fort Worth, Texas, one of the 24 plants named by Mr. Collins, took a number of undisclosed safeguards against infiltration by SDS.

A spokesman for General Electric said the company had alerted the employee-relations managers in all of its 180 plants and had supplied each with a copy of the SDS manual. (The text of the manual is published in the appendix of this book.)

The exact number of students who secured "work-in" jobs has never been established. SDS sources put the figure anywhere between 1,000 and 2,000. They claimed that nearly every student who joined the campaign was able to land a job.

The outcome did not appear to be very successful. A survey of 16 major cities produced no evidence of violence or worker-student confrontations.

SDS leader Mark Rudd said: "Lots of stuff happened in streets with working class youths, but not so much in shops."

A spokesman for the FBI said: "They weren't too successful. Industries were warned ahead of time."

The student extremists had to face opposition from trade unions as well as from employers. An official of the United Auto Workers union said the students would be "eaten alive" by workers once they discovered that the summer transients were Marxists.

The attitude of many workers also was reflected by Karl F. Feller, president of the Brewery Workers union, who said: "A well-placed fist could be the welcome that awaits SDS revolutionaries."

Nevertheless, Alan Spector, an SDS official, was quoted as having said: "But we do have a lot of people on the inside now, and the workers listen to us. We make it clear we're not there to use them but to join in smashing the oppressive system. The ruling class is scared silly now, and it should be."

In the two other areas—joining picketing strikers and helping black unions—there was more visible evidence of success.

Students of the University of West Virginia joined West Virginia coal miners who went out on strike to protest allegedly inadequate protective measures against "black lung" disease.

In San Francisco, students of the State College helped man the picket line during a strike against a refinery of the Standard Oil Company of California. The workers, in return, helped the students picket the college.

In Mahwah, New Jersey, students joined members of the United

Black Brotherhood, who had called a wildcat strike at the local Ford Motor Company plant allegedly because a supervisor had cursed a black worker. White workers failed to support the walk-out, and the strike collapsed after a week. Nevertheless, the black strike leader was enthusiastic over the participation of the students.

Discrimination against blacks by predominantly white trade unions has played into the hands of extremists who are now active in organizing exclusively black labor unions. A counterpart of the United Black Brotherhood, the Dodge Revolutionary Union Movement, is active among auto workers in Detroit. In New York City, a black group is trying to displace the Transport Workers union as the representative for city transit workers.

Members of the United Black Brothers, the Black Panthers, and the SDS helping strikers picket at the Mahwah, New Jersey, plant of the Ford Motor Company.

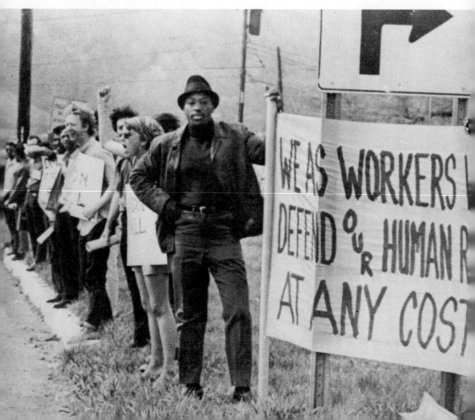

Marxists have become aware of a potentially fruitful field of industrial penetration right on the campus where they are going to school. They have declared their intention of indoctrinating and winning over students who are studying to be engineers, chemists, doctors, and technicians in all fields of science. These students later will hold key positions in industry and science. Those who had been converted to Marxism could conceivably become valuable allies for a revolutionary movement.

However, for the present, Marxist students appear to be a long way from reaching the point where, as in the case of the Sorbonne students, they could trigger a national explosion. This is not due to a shortcoming on their part. American students, on the whole, have probably been more active than the French. It is due, rather, to the weakness of the Communist Party. Whereas the American students may be in a position to supply a fuse, the Communist Party is not in a position to supply a charge of organized labor required for an explosion.

In France, students could touch off an uprising because the French Communist Party, controlling the bulk of organized labor, could deliver the essential element for such an undertaking. In the United States, the Communist Party has virtually disappeared as a factor in organized labor.

This was not always the case. In the 1930s, communists and their sympathizers controlled many key posts in the newly organized Congress of Industrial Organizations, and it aspired to securing control of individual craft unions within the American Federation of Labor.

The AFL leadership was determined to prevent communist penetration, and at its 1939 convention put through a resolution stating "that we instruct the various affiliated national and international unions to refrain from taking into membership any known member of the Communist Party, or any sympathizer."

Communists made some headway in Hollywood, where they established the Conference of Studio Unions under the leadership of Herbert K. Sorrell. But their success in the movie industry was slight compared with their achievements in the CIO.

John L. Lewis, dynamic head of the United Mine Workers of

America, was the guiding hand behind formation of the CIO after
its members broke away from the AFL, and he became its first
president. Represented at the first CIO convention in November
1938 at Pittsburgh were 32 national and international unions. It
was time, said Lewis, to organize on an industrywide basis.

Lewis had fought bitter battles against communists for control of
the United Mine Workers. But in the early days of the CIO, he and
other founders felt they needed all the help they could get. They
let word out that they had no objection to communists joining their
movement. At first, the communists wanted no part of the CIO:
"We communists say that the struggle of the workers to organize
must be carried on within the AF of L regardless of its reactionary
leadership for it is here that the great mass of organized workers
are to be found."

But the communists quickly realized that the CIO was going to
survive. And with a leadership that appeared receptive to communist participation it seemed ripe for full-scale penetration. Soon
communists occupied several key posts. Michael Quill, for example,
was head of the Transport Workers union and also leader of the
New York Metropolitan Industrial Union Council. Harry Bridges,
Australian-born communist, head of the West coast longshoremen's
union, was in charge of the California CIO. Joseph Curran, another
communist sympathizer, became head of the Atlantic and Gulf
coast seamen. With Bridges and Curran on their side, the communists controlled some of the most influential segments of the
maritime unions.

Other communist dominated unions within the CIO included the
International Union of Mine, Mill and Smelter Workers, the United
Farm Equipment and Metal Workers union, and the United Office
and Professional Workers of America. The latter union played a key
role because it supplied office workers for most union headquarters.
When Lewis learned that members of the office workers union were
handing confidential files over to Communist Party members, he
issued a warning to regional directors not to hire communists.

Communists also tried to win over Homer Martin, president of
the United Auto Workers. They offered to wage a campaign to
boost his prestige within the CIO. But Martin turned them down

A rare photograph of the turbulent national convention of the Students for a Democratic Society, held in Chicago in 1969 to elect new leaders and to decide new programs of action. The "capitalistic press" was barred, and this picture was taken by an amateur photographer. SDS was deeply fractured as a result of struggle for power among three groups. Anarchistic RYM I defeated Maoist PLP and anti-PLP, Maoist RYM II.

and they bitterly opposed him afterward.

Until the signing of the Nazi-Soviet Pact in 1939, Communist dominated unions had been ardent supporters of a popular front against fascism. But after the pact was signed, they adhered to the international communist line and came out strongly against American participation in the war against Germany. The New York Seamen's and Harbor Workers branch of the Communist Party described the outbreak of the war in Europe as "an imperialist war for profits, markets and colonies. The American working people have nothing to gain and everything to lose by American participation in this war."

The line shifted dramatically, of course, after the Nazi invasion of Russia on June 22, 1941. Lewis was attacked by the communists for his refusal to forget wage increases for miners.

Communist influence in the American labor movement nevertheless survived the twists and turns of Soviet foreign policy in the late 1930s. It was in the immediate postwar period that communist influence started to slide downhill. Postwar policies of the Soviet Union disillusioned many Americans who had felt friendly toward the Russians. More importantly for the labor movement, many CIO leaders who once felt they needed communist help to keep control of their unions now were secure.

Both Quill and Curran dropped their communist affiliations and became leaders of the movement to drive communists out of the CIO.

The fight between communist and anticommunist forces within the CIO reached a climax at the federation's 1949 convention. By then Philip Murray had taken over as president of the CIO. The key battle would be between the federation and the United Electrical Workers, largest of the communist dominated unions.

A resolution introduced at the convention said, "We can no longer tolerate within the family of the CIO the communist party masquerading as a labor union."

In an impassioned speech, Murray told the delegates: "I have asked these so-called apostles of democracy to stand somewhere, sometime on the floor of a national convention of the CIO and to criticize the Cominform, or criticize Russia's policy of expansionism, to criticize any of the policies of Russia, and these hypocrites run from me. They dare not stand upon their dirty feet and give any expression of opposition to anything the Soviets are doing."

The convention voted to expel the United Electrical, Radio and Machine Workers. It also amended the federation constitution to bar communists from serving as officers or members of the executive board.

During the following year all the communist dominated unions were expelled and many of them dissolved after their membership was raided by both the AFL and the CIO.

For a brief period, communists threatened to become a major force in the American labor movement, a force possibly comparable to the one they hold in European countries. But they failed

Harry Bridges (left) president of the International Longshoremen's and Warehousemen's Union, is one of the few remnants of former left-wing strength in the U.S. labor movement. Michael J. Quill (center) once represented communist strength in the U.S. labor movement but today, as international president of the Transport Workers Union, stands as a bulwark against communist influence and evidence of communist defeat on the U.S. labor front. Joseph Curran (right) also became disillusioned both with the Soviet Union and U.S. Communists, joining the campaign to drive the latter out of the U.S. trade union movement.

because the American worker discovered that he could get what he wanted not through revolution, led by the Communist Party, but through negotiations or strikes, led by his noncommunist trade union.

And so long as that is the case, both the Old and the New Left will have trouble in getting the American worker to produce a Marxist revolution for them.

Chapter Eight

Spying for Russia

The international scope of communism has given the Soviet Union a unique advantage in the shadowy world of spying. In nearly every country of the world there is a communist movement, however small. And it is often from dedicated believers in the teachings of Marx and Lenin that the Soviets have been able to recruit willing and able undercover agents.

All countries seek information about other nations, particularly potential enemies. Much information is easy to come by, as simple as reading the daily newspapers. But there is a great deal, such as military secrets, that can be very difficult to obtain. It often requires the efforts of trained espionage agents, who must recruit people holding sensitive positions in government.

There are hazards to recruiting. It is almost impossible for an agent to be absolutely certain that the man he is recruiting is not a counterintelligence operator.

For years, Soviet agents in the United States tried a short cut by looking to the Communist Party-U.S.A. for recruits or information on likely prospects. It was common practice that when an agent was recruited from the party he resigned and severed all contacts with party members to improve his chances of escaping detection.

Two of the most successful agents of this sort were Julius and

Ethel Rosenberg, who played key roles in obtaining American atomic secrets for the Russians. Both had been party members, and they cut loose from the party when they became part of a Soviet spy ring.

The party also could supply Soviet agents with the names of trusted people holding special skills and connections. For example, an agent who needed a skilled shortwave radio operator could rely on the party to steer him to someone likely to be trustworthy. Party members also were used to establish business fronts through which funds and stolen information could be channeled.

Just how extensively Soviet agents depended on the party is shown by FBI files which record that in one major spy ring 12 of the 17 members had been in the Communist Party.

But that dependence lessened rapidly when Soviet intelligence discovered the extent of FBI infiltration of the American Communist Party. It eventually learned that many party members were working for the FBI. That seriously undermined the value of the party as a channel for intelligence operations.

U.S. counterintelligence officials believe that Soviet intelligence agents have largely abandoned the party as one of their instruments. They believe that Soviet agents look elsewhere for recruits.

The ideal recruit is an individual ideologically committed to communism who has never made his beliefs well known and who has never joined the Communist Party. Harry Gold was such a man. Gold was a key figure in the Rosenberg atomic spy ring.

There were many others, people who came to believe, often during the depression years, that Karl Marx had been right about the "evils" of capitalism. In their desire to work for what they thought was a better system, some of these people took government jobs in the hope of bringing about changes by working within the system. In the case of others, the reasons were more sinister. They deliberately took government employment in an effort to gain access to information that would be useful to the Soviet Union.

Whatever their reasons for entering government service, World War II moved many of these people to try to help the Soviet Union. After the Nazi invasion of Russia in 1941, the Soviet Union suddenly became an ally of the anti-German coalition. Stories of the heroic

Ethel and Julius Rosenberg arrive for trial after being charged with conspiring to deliver U.S. national defense secrets to the Russians. They were executed as atomic spies in 1953.

battles fought by the Red Army made many people forget communism and its aims. The immediate view was that of a country fighting for its life against Nazi tyranny.

Some who felt an ideological kinship with the Soviet Union attempted to help the Russians by passing American military secrets to them. The Rosenbergs, for example, headed one ring which succeeded in obtaining top secret information on radar. Many such rings operated in the United States. The FBI estimates that during the war years 18 Soviet spy rings were functioning in the United States.

How many are operating now? And where do they get their recruits?

No one knows for certain how many undercover spy rings are operating in the United States today. J. Edgar Hoover described the problem briefly in an appearance before a Congressional committee. "Once a deep-cover agent has gained entry to our country," Hoover said, "he easily becomes assimilated into our vast population under an assumed identity. His detection and identification at this point become a counter-intelligence problem of extreme magnitude."

As for the question of whether there are any at all, Hoover said, "FBI sources clearly indicate no letup on the part of the communist countries in their intelligence attacks against the United States for the purpose of penetrating our national defense interests."

Just as it is impossible to say how many espionage rings may be operating in the United States, so too is it impossible to declare with certainty that Soviet agents have ceased entirely using the services of known leftists. The only certain clues the public has about the sort of people recruited have come from exposure of espionage operations. Exposure of such operations in recent years has not turned up party members or New Leftists. Most often the Americans involved have been members of the military who were drawn into a spy ring through blackmail or greed.

Military personnel are a common target because of their access to information sought by intelligence operatives. Past cases also indicate that approaches often are made to persons who may have relatives behind the Iron Curtain.

Technological advances have enabled both sides in the Cold War to shift some of the work of intelligence gathering to satellites, planes, and ships, all loaded with sensitive electronic gear. But much of the work still must be done by people. And embassies provide a convenient base for many of these operations.

One Soviet defector estimated that 70 to 80 percent of the people on communist embassy staffs work in intelligence.

There are advantages to using a diplomatic mission as a base for intelligence agents. The embassy provides an area which authorities of the host country cannot enter or search without permission. Diplomatic pouches also are immune from search. And members of the diplomatic corps have immunity from arrest or prosecution. If caught spying, the worst that can happen to a diplomat is that he will be forced to leave the country.

But there also are disadvantages. Diplomatic personnel from unfriendly countries are watched closely by counterintelligence agents. To make it easier for us to keep track of the movements of Soviet diplomats they must file detailed travel plans if they intend to go more than 25 miles from Washington. The same restriction applies to American diplomats in Moscow. Both the United States and the Soviet Union bar diplomats from traveling to certain areas.

Whether they are intelligence agents filling a slot on an embassy staff or deep cover agents who have entered the country on forged papers, the chief problem still is recruiting.

For the cautious agent, aware of the potential pitfalls, recruiting is a long process, often taking years. At first, the target is cultivated socially. He suddenly finds he has a new friend who seems to be a very pleasant companion. After a while, the friend may ask for a favor. Would it be possible for him to obtain a harmless bit of information, nothing classified? If that is supplied, there might be other, similar requests. The friend insists that the individual accept some payment in return for his trouble. Then he finds he has been compromised. He has accepted payment from a foreign power for information. From then on the requests are likely to concern far more serious material.

There are other ways to compromise an individual and draw

him into an intelligence network. Master Sergeant Roy Adair
Rhodes was entrapped while working as chief of the U.S. embassy
garage in Moscow. One day, two Russian nationals employed as
mechanics invited Rhodes to join them for a drink.

Despite warnings that all Russians employed in foreign embassies were probably intelligence agents, Rhodes accepted their
invitation. He later testified that "one drink led to another and
it went on all afternoon." Soon, two girls joined them and the
whole group went out to have dinner and more drinks.

The next morning, Rhodes woke up in bed with one of the
girls. Several weeks later she called Rhodes and asked to meet
him. She told the sergeant, who was married and had one child,
that she was pregnant.

The Soviets offered Rhodes a way out. All he had to do was
to obtain certain information from the embassy. He agreed and
was paid between $2,500 and $3,000 for the material he turned
over to the Russians. Later, he was caught, convicted of conspiracy to commit espionage, and sentenced to five years in prison.

Soviet embassy officials in Washington hoped that friendship,
an East European background, and a thirst for profit would help
them get information from a local businessman.

John Huminik, Jr., an expert in metallurgy and rocketry, was
secretary of the American Society of Metals when he first met
Dr. Sergei Stupar, a scientist on the Soviet embassy staff. Stupar
applied for membership in the society, whose ranks included
scientists from about 20 countries.

Soon Huminik found himself being invited to embassy receptions as well as quiet dinners at the homes of members of the
staff. Huminik later told Congressional committees "they pro-
ceeded to evaluate me . . . asking me for simple reports that were
difficult to obtain but unclassified."

At a meeting in a Washington restaurant, Vladimir Zorov, an
embassy third secretary, told Huminik, "We would be glad to pay
very good prices for any information you could give to our government. We take care of our friends; we also take care of our
enemies."

Huminik's father had been born in Russia. At one meeting, Dr.

Stupar told Huminik, "We found relatives of yours in the Georgian part of Russia." The matter never was raised again after Huminik replied, "Get off that. I don't have any relatives that mean anything to me anyway and just forget it."

What sort of information did the Russians want? "They basically wanted scientific and engineering reports," said Huminik:

> They want technology, new weapons, faster airplanes, rockets, things like that. They wanted proprietary industrial processes, such as the oxygen steel process as installed in this country. They wanted details—what size pipe is used, the pressures, the operational details so they could duplicate. . . . They wanted records of classified technical meetings or conferences during this period and they asked me to go and get the proceedings or to order the proceedings later and pass it on to them.

Harry Gold (upper left) was convicted as an atomic spy in 1950; Roy A. Rhodes (right) was blackmailed into his espionage activities; and John Huminik, Jr., (lower left) was a successful double agent.

One of Huminik's embassy contacts, Valentin Revin, pressed
him for information about the U.S. Surveyor moon program.
Huminik said Revin told him "he was highly interested in the
Surveyor moon probe and his government wanted me to have
this as my top priority....He wanted me to find specific data....
He knew what was classified and what he needed and he wanted
me to get it and put it in a drop on a certain date."

In the spy business a "drop" is a place where one agent leaves
material for another to pick up. "The places we had the dead
drops would be like the base of a tree, a sign post, a dump area
where you had a 'No Dumping' sign, or wooded area," Huminik
said. After leaving material at a drop, Huminik was told to go
to a particular telephone booth and mark a specific page in the
telephone book with a number ending in three zeroes. That
would be a sign to a Soviet contact that material had been left
at the drop.

The Russians made other promises: "They promised me forged
passports to get out of the country should I get caught by the
FBI," Huminik said. "They promised trade agreements and they
also gave me money." They also told Huminik that "a person
with my talents in many fields would be well taken care of in
Russia and that I would have everything that I needed."

But Huminik was one of those cases intelligence operatives
dread. From the very first contacts with the Soviets, he had con-
sulted with the FBI and cooperated in gathering evidence to
expose the embassy network.

When a Soviet diplomat is caught in espionage activity, the
State Department sends off a note such as this:

> The Secretary of State presents his compliments to His
> Excellency the Ambassador of the Union of Soviet Socialist
> Republics, and states the following:
>
> The government of the United States has ascertained that
> Yuri V. Novikov, Second Secretary of the embassy, has en-
> gaged in activities incompatible with his status as an accredited
> diplomatic official.
>
> Therefore, this government is impelled to declare Mr. Novi-

kov persona non grata. The embassy is requested to make arrangements for his immediate departure from the United States.

In the tit for tat world of international diplomacy, the expulsion of a Russian by the United States is certain to be followed by similar action by the Soviets against an American of equal rank in the U.S. embassy in Moscow. The same thing happens when the Russians catch one of our diplomatic intelligence agents.

We spy on the Russians; the Russians spy on us. But it's not an even contest. The difference is in the nature of our societies. The Soviet government feels no obligation to supply a great deal of important information to its people. Ours does.

Secretary of State Dean Rusk explained it this way in an appearance before the Senate Foreign Relations Committee: "We in this country have an open society where 99.9 percent of the total information about our country is open to the public. Our approach to security and to classified information is that we cannot close up a society but that we try to protect the information, whether it is a particular military installation or classified material in the hands of the government."

A former communist embassy official who later defected to the West agrees with Rusk. Powel Monat served as Air and Naval Attache in the Polish embassy in Washington. His primary assignment was to collect intelligence information.

He estimates that 95 percent of the material useful to foreign intelligence analysts can be obtained legally in the United States. Furthermore, says Monat, 90 percent of the time of an intelligence agent in any other country would be spent trying to obtain, illegally, information that is readily available in the United States.

Where does all this material come from?

Copies of patents on file for industrial machinery and processes can be purchased for 25 cents each. The Soviet embassy once ordered copies of 41,812 patents. Their next order was for 41,810.

To learn about port facilities in the United States, one need only go to the Government Printing Office in Washington to buy an 18-volume report by the U.S. Army Corps of Engineers.

Want to know about U.S. airports, large and small? The government sells pilot's handbooks containing detailed information about airports including diagrams and the approaches used for landings.

Public scientific meetings are good sources on up-to-date developments in many fields. The FBI reports that it watched two Soviet embassy officials at a Western Electric convention in Los Angeles. The Russians methodically collected every bit of literature available. By the time they finished, the FBI estimates they took about 250 pounds of documents.

Then there are the many trade magazines which regularly report the latest developments in such industries as aircraft and aerospace. Monat tried to subscribe to *Aviation Week* but was turned down because of his position with the Polish embassy. Still, he could walk into the magazine's main office in New York City and buy all the back copies he wanted.

Communist diplomats can use all the sources listed above without getting into any trouble, but there are some limitations. For example, Soviet citizens are prohibited from obtaining aerial photographs except where they "appear in or are appendices to newspapers, periodicals, technical journals, atlases and books commercially available to the general public."

Vast areas of the country are covered by aerial photos available to the general public. FBI files show many cases of Soviet embassy officials buying aerial photos from legitimate sources. Two Russian embassy officials bought 15 aerial photos of the Minneapolis–St. Paul area. Two others bought aerial photos on one trip to Dallas, Tulsa, Fort Worth, and the surrounding areas in which are located a Naval air station, an Army air field, and an Air Force base. Similar purchases have been made of photos showing Boston; Long Island, New York; Newport, Rhode Island; and Los Angeles.

However, the photos needed aren't always available to the general public. Leonid Pivnev, an assistant air attache at the Soviet embassy, ran into this problem when he was ordered to obtain aerial photos of New York City that would show certain port areas, industrial facilities, and military installations. Unable to find them commercially available, Pivnev asked a Washington photographer to take them. The photographer reported the incident and Pivnev was asked to leave the country.

On another occasion, the offending diplomat, Nikolai Trofimov, was stationed with the Soviet embassy in Mexico City. Trofimov tried to hire an American photographer to take aerial photos of 45 U.S. cities. Nineteen of those cities were located near Strategic Air Command bases. The other 26 had either key industrial complexes or military bases nearby.

It becomes less and less likely each year that the Russians will have to bother any longer trying to hire American photographers. For they, like the United States, are shifting such jobs to satellites which, while circling the globe at an altitude of about 100 miles, can take remarkable photos of the land below. Such satellites are revolutionizing this aspect of intelligence gathering.

U.S. officials have acknowledged that the electronic equipment on one new American spy satellite is capable of locating Soviet missile bases, giving instant warning when a missile is launched, and telling what type missile it is.

Before the satellites were developed, the American U-2 plane was the most effective spy in the sky. Developed to operate at extremely high altitudes out of range of antiaircraft weapons then in existence, the U-2 made many trips over Russia and China in the 1950s. But in 1960, Soviet antiaircraft finally caught up with the U-2. One piloted by Francis Gary Powers was shot down over the Soviet Union. Powers lived, and enough of his plane survived to reveal to the Russians the purpose of his mission. Suddenly, the world became aware of this new, sophisticated form of spying.

What sort of people have been the most effective spies for the communists?

When Colonel Rudolph Ivanovich Abel, Soviet master spy, was unmasked and thrust into public view, he bore little physical resemblance to the dashing heroes of spy novels. The man the American public saw looked a lot like a school teacher. Tall, thin, and balding, Abel was well into middle age. He was a man who could melt easily into a crowd.

It may have been hard for some Americans to picture this mild-looking man as a threat to American security. Yet for nearly 10 years, Abel was one of the most successful Soviet agents in the United States. He headed a nationwide network of communist agents that concentrated on obtaining U.S. military and atomic secrets. Abel worked so effectively, so unobtrusively, that it was only through the defection of one of his aides that the colonel was finally caught.

The indictment handed down by a federal grand jury charged that Abel conspired to "agree to communicate, deliver and transmit to . . . the Union of Soviet Socialist Republics . . . documents, writing, photographs, photographic negatives, plans, maps, models, instruments, appliances and information relating to the national defense of the United States of America, and particularly information relating to the arms, equipment and disposition of the United States Armed Forces, and information relating to the atomic energy program of the United States."

It also charged that Abel would "activate and attempt to activate as agents within the United States certain members of the armed forces who were in a position to acquire information relating to the national defense."

James B. Donovan was Abel's lawyer. Soon after he took the case, Donovan called a news conference at which he contrasted Abel and Americans who betrayed their country to spy for the Soviet Union. "If the government's allegations are true," said Donovan, "it means that instead of dealing with Americans who have betrayed their country, we have here a Russian citizen, in a quasi-military capacity, who has served his country on an extraordinarily dangerous mission."

Donovan later told a story to illustrate Abel's loyalty to his homeland. The Russian secret service colonel told Donovan that after he was arrested the FBI offered him freedom and a $10,000-a-year job in U.S. counterintelligence if he would switch sides in the Cold War. Donovan quoted Abel as saying, "They must think all of us are rats who can be bought."

Of the Soviet agent who betrayed him, Abel told his lawyer,

"I can't understand how a man, to save his own skin, would betray his country and place his family in complete dishonor at home."

Abel was an extraordinary man. He was fluent in six languages, was an electronics engineer, and had a working knowledge of chemistry, physics, and mathematics. He also was a talented painter and guitar player.

He entered Canada from Europe with papers identifying him as Emil R. Goldfus, a displaced person of German-Irish ancestry. Then he crossed the border illegally into the United States. Once across the border, Abel went to New York City and opened a small photographic studio in Brooklyn. Then he set about contacting the network of agents he was to head.

A cautious, highly-trained professional, Abel took great pains to avoid personal contact with members of his spy network. Information was rarely, if ever, passed from hand to hand. Drops were set up throughout the New York area with hollowed out coins, jewelry, bolts, and other objects used as containers for microfilm.

After Abel was caught, the Soviet government refused even to acknowledge that there was such a man. But that didn't bother Abel. It was one of the rules of his profession.

Upon conviction, Abel faced a possible death sentence. Donovan argued successfully against the death penalty and he was given 30 years in prison. Donovan's argument had been based primarily on the possibility that the government might someday want to exchange Abel for an American caught spying in the Soviet Union. And it turned out that Abel was exchanged for Francis Gary Powers, the U-2 pilot.

The Soviet Union has a rigorous training course for developing agents like Abel. The first stop is the Marx-Engels school at Gorki. Many more schools and assignments follow during a training period that can last as long as 10 years. At any stage along the way, candidates who fail to meet the rigorous standards are dropped from the course.

Those who make it have received instruction in every facet of their new trade. They learn the use and handling of explosives and firearms, drugs, and poisons. They are taught shortwave radio operation and photography. They are indoctrinated in the language and customs of the Western countries to which they might be sent.

Donovan quotes Abel as expressing dismay at how anyone could betray his country. Yet the people professionals such as Abel depended upon for the success of their missions were those willing to be traitors.

Harry Gold, a key figure in the Rosenberg atom spy ring, is an example. Gold was to give a description of the life of a spy that was as far from James Bond as it could be:

> The difficulty of raising money for . . . trips; the weary hours of waiting on streetcorners in strange towns where I had no business to be and the killing of time in cheap movies; and the lies I had to tell at home and to my friends to explain my supposed whereabouts—Mom was certain I was carrying on a series of clandestine love affairs. It was drudgery . . . any who had an idea this work was glamorous and exciting was very wrong indeed—nothing could have been more dreary.

What made Gold accept this dreary, dangerous existence? Why did he risk so much to help the Soviet Union? Because, he said, he had "a genuine desire to help the people of the Soviet Union to be able to enjoy some of the better things of life. . . . Here, too, in the person of the Soviet Union, was the one bulwark against the further encroachment of that monstrosity, fascism. . . . Anything that was against anti-semitism I was for, and so the chance to help strengthen the Soviet Union seemed like a wonderful opportunity."

Others gave other reasons for betrayal. Dr. Allan Nunn May, a British physicist, was involved in the same ring as Gold and the Rosenbergs. In a confession dictated after he was caught, May recalled his decision: "I gave and had given very careful consideration to correctness of making sure that development of atomic energy was not confined to U.S.A. I took the very painful decision that it was necessary to convey general information on atomic energy and make sure it was taken seriously. For this reason I decided to entertain a proposition made to me by the individual who called on me."

Dr. Klaus Fuchs, another physicist involved in the atom spy plot, had been a communist since his youth. Nevertheless, he explained—

In the postwar period I began again to have my doubts about the Russian policy. It is almost impossible to give definite incidents, because now the control mechanism acted against me also, keeping away from me facts which I could not look in the face; but they did penetrate and eventually I came to the point where I knew I disapproved of the Russian government and of the Communist Party. But I still believed that

Colonel Rudolph Abel (upper left), Leonid Pivnev (right), and Klaus Fuchs (lower left) each spied for the Soviets with a greater or lesser degree of success until they were uncovered.

they would build a new world and that one day I would take part in it.

Thus, some of the most valuable espionage agents who betray their countries to the Soviet Union are those who fall victim to illusions about the purity, idealism, and goodness of the Soviet state. In the creation of these illusions, the communist parties of the United States and other Western countries have played and continue to play a most important role.

Chapter Nine

The Left and the Law

Buildings are seized. Campuses are paralyzed. Draft records are destroyed. Demonstrators and police clash. In the aftermath, courts must decide the right of Americans to protest as well as their right to protection from demonstrators.

Where is the line to be drawn between the right to protest and the right to be protected? How far can the protestors go?

Does a belief that the Vietnam war is immoral justify pouring blood on Selective Service records? Or storming the Pentagon? Or disrupting the public appearances of government officials who support the war?

Does a belief that university administrators are blind to the legitimate grievances of students justify taking control of a building and wrecking the furniture? Or disrupting the classes of professors who disagree with the protestors' views?

Does a belief that a practice that prohibits whites and Negroes from sitting at the same lunch counter is wrong justify disrupting the business of that counter?

These are among the questions courts have dealt with or will decide in the near future. There also are challenges to government policy: for example, can the government legally draft Vietnam war protestors ahead of other people?

Throughout history dissenters have found it necessary to challenge laws they thought unjust. To protest the U.S. declaration of war on Mexico in 1846, Henry David Thoreau, philosopher and writer, refused to pay his poll tax and spent a night in the Concord, Massachusetts, jail.

More than a century later, young idealists who took Thoreau for one of their heroes invaded the South to challenge laws upholding racial segregation. The brutal response to the nonviolent demonstrators by authorities in many southern communities aroused the nation. Congress acted to outlaw racial segregation in public accommodations.

Civil disobedience brought progress for the Negro in the South. The civil rights leaders who practiced it kept it nonviolent and under control.

But in the hands of the extreme left, civil disobedience has taken a new turn. No longer is the target an unjust law. The target is the structure of society. No longer are the demonstrators nonviolent. Now they seek to provoke violence, disorder, and disruption.

What is the attitude of the Communist Party-U.S.A. and the New Left toward the American system of law? Are they willing to work within it to achieve their goals?

According to Communist Party leaders, American communists are the true upholders of the constitution. The party platform proclaims: "We communists are defenders of the Constitution in principle and practice."

The platform further declares: "It strikes us as folly to think that monopoly can be overcome and revolutionary transformation of society be undertaken without the sanction and participation of a majority of the [American] people." Thus the party presents itself as an advocate of democracy, an upholder of the law.

But is that a true picture? Has party leader Gus Hall changed so much since the day he testified that he would willingly take up arms to overthrow the government? Or does the party attitude toward American law and the Constitution depend on the current line as dictated by Moscow?

Historically, the communist attitude toward the law has been marked by cynicism. The party has taken advantage of, even demanded, all the protection available under the Constitution, while at the same time vowing to overthrow the system whose protection it seeks.

The party used the protection of the law to fight a long and ultimately successful battle against two laws designed to destroy it. The first, the Smith Act, made it a federal crime to advocate the overthrow of the government by force and violence. The second required the party to register as a communist action group controlled by the Soviet Union.

In a long series of trials, over 130 party members were convicted of violating the Smith Act. Most of the top party leaders were sentenced to terms in federal prisons. Eventually the Supreme Court found most sections of the Smith Act in violation of constitutional guarantees of free speech.

During their trials, the communists tried to walk a very fine legal line. Claude Lightfoot described it in a pamphlet aimed at convincing militant Negroes that the party was not against violence. Lightfoot wrote: "Throughout the Smith Act trials we communists never renounced force and violence per se. We said that at certain historical moments the necessity for armed struggle may be present. But we held that we were not guilty of a conspiracy to employ force and violence, nor were we guilty of teaching and advocating the necessity of the overthrow of the government by force and violence."

The registration requirement was fought through the courts by the party until ultimately the Supreme Court declared that the law violated constitutional protections against self-incrimination. Those two guarantees, the First and Fifth Amendments to the Constitution, have a long history of use by communists. Congressional committee records are filled with cases of known or suspected communists who declined to answer any questions on the grounds of possible self-incrimination.

In 1968, the party turned its attention to election laws, particularly those aimed at keeping subversives off the ballot. In Illinois, for example, Jack Kling, secretary of the state communist party and a candidate for the legislature, refused to sign a loyalty oath required of candidates. Kling argued that the loyalty oath was a "denial of the right to communists and other political minority groups to be candidates for public office."

Loyalty oaths such as the one required in Illinois present a traditional problem to the Communist Party in its current effort to gain acceptance as just another minority party in America. Loyalty oaths have always been a party target because they expose party members to perjury charges if they sign. The party could argue, as it did in the Smith Act cases, that it does not advocate violent overthrow of the government, that it would resort to violence only if the government resisted the desire of the majority to change the system. While it might be successful with such an argument, it would be involved, once again, in long and costly litigation. Kling's challenge of the Illinois loyalty oath failed, but the party scored a victory in Minnesota.

In that state, the party went into federal court in an effort to put its presidential ticket on the ballot. State election officials had refused to list the communist ticket on the grounds that the action would violate the federal Subversive Activities Control Act. The party scored an easy victory in this case when U.S. Attorney General Ramsay Clark notified the court that it was the opinion of the government that giving the party a place on the ballot would not violate federal law. Its victory in Minnesota gave the party a place on the ballots in two states. They were listed on the state of Washington ballot without a fight.

Communist Party dealings with the law have been systematic and in recent years confined to courtrooms and congressional hearing rooms. New Left approaches to the law are far less organized and far more wideranging.

Like the Communist Party, the New Left seeks the protection given dissenters by American law. However, it goes much farther than the party in using lawbreaking as a form of protest. New Left groups such as SDS that use disruption as a means of achieving their immediate goals raise questions of what rights the majority have to protection against such tactics.

Attorney General John N. Mitchell described the attitude recently when he said:

It seems to me that the danger today comes from those who justify physical violence—not as sporadic or symbolic protest as did Thoreau—but as the only form of protest; as the only consistent and acceptable method of forcing their demands upon the majority.

There are those on our college campuses who argue that administrators will listen only after buildings are seized and students injured.

There are those among our black community who argue that the white community will listen only after arson and looting have occurred.

There are those in our urban areas who argue that the dropout juvenile mugger and the disadvantaged adult bandit are, in some unconscious way, bringing to our attention their plight.

Jerry Rubin, Yippie leader, hammers a point at a press conference, with six others accused of conspiracy to incite mob action at the Democratic National Convention in Chicago. The six, standing behind Rubin, are (left to right) John Froines, Abbie Hoffman, Lee Weiner, David Dellinger, Thomas Hayden, and Rennie Davis. Mrs. Rubin is seated next to her husband.

Recently college campuses have been the scene of a steadily accelerating trend toward violent protest, led usually by the New Left. By the close of the 1968-69 school year, more than 250 schools had been the scene of violent protests. The disturbances resulted in the arrest of more than 3,000 persons and property damage totaling more than $2 million.

Early in 1969, the Supreme Court dealt with two cases involving protests by students. A key factor in the decisions was whether the protest was disruptive. The court ruled that a group of Iowa school children had a right to wear black armbands to school to protest the Vietnam war over their teachers' objection. "It can hardly be argued," said the court, "that either students or teachers shed their constitutional rights to freedom of speech or expression at the schoolhouse gate." The court emphasized that the protest was "unaccompanied by any disorder or disturbance."

Two weeks later, the court rejected the contention of 10 West Virginia college students that they had a right to an impartial trial before being suspended from school for participating in a demonstration at Bluefield State College, West Virginia. After first demonstrating at a football game, the students followed Wendell G. Hardway, the college president, to a parking lot and rocked and beat on his automobile.

In that opinion, the court said that students who engage in an "aggressive and violent demonstration" are not protected by the First Amendment. They were suspended justly for "violent and destructive interference with the rights of others."

In the disorganized, undisciplined ranks of the New Left, there is no party-line approach to the law. The tactics of disruption are a standard device. What happens when New Leftists come in direct conflict with the courts? The response can be hard to predict. In some cases, the respect for courts that most Americans grow up with comes to the fore.

Among hard-core extremists, on the other hand, the courts are a tool of the capitalist system they are determined to overthrow. To them a court order is an act of repression. Defiance of such an order is a revolutionary act.

State University of New York at Stony Brook, Long Island, has

President Wendell G. Hardway (left) of Bluefield State College, West Virginia, examines bomb damage to the college's physical education building.

been the scene of a number of demonstrations led by SDS. When 120 students occupied the university computer center and declared that it was being used for defense research, Dr. John S. Toll, university president, went to court. Within hours he had obtained a restraining order and the students quietly left the building.

But at Howard University in Washington, D.C., black students took over six buildings in defiance of a court order. Later, a number of students were charged with contempt. Two pleaded guilty in federal district court and were sentenced to six months in jail. All but two weeks of that sentence was suspended.

The other students escaped prosecution after a full-page advertisement was run in local newspapers giving the university administration's side of the story. Defense counsel charged that the advertisement, running as it did during the trial of three of the students, would prevent them from getting a fair trial. The judge agreed and dismissed charges.

The idea of making even more widespread use of injunctions is one solution to campus unrest that is under consideration by the Nixon administration. The plan would have Congress authorize a college to get a federal court injunction to halt a student demonstration or prohibit a planned protest.

Carl Davidson, a leader of SDS, suggested in an article that campus radicals form a student defense league to help resist university disciplinary efforts. "The purpose of the group," he wrote, "would be to make its services available to any student who must appear before campus authorities for infractions of repressive (or just plain stupid) rules and regulations." Then he added, "It might be wise to include law students or local radical lawyers in the group for the purpose of making legal counter-attacks."

Few clashes between universities and their students have reached higher federal courts. The West Virginia case was the first involving a conflict between a university and its students to reach the Supreme Court since 1934. So far, school administrators have tried to use internal procedures for dealing with demonstrators. In doing so they have raised other questions we will soon examine, concerning enforcement of the law.

The Vietnam war, on the other hand, has raised many legal issues and has been the target of legal assaults from the left.

In an effort to use legal points as a weapon in their attacks on the war, leftists and other opponents of U.S. involvement in Vietnam argued that the war had been escalated without the consent of Congress and therefore was illegal. Extremists also tried to use what they called the immorality of the war as justification for illegal forms of protest.

U.S. Attorney Stephen H. Sachs referred to this tactic in his statement at the sentencing of nine Roman Catholic clergymen and laymen. "What crimes can we permit to be committed in the name of sincerity?" asked Sachs. "What they did is precisely the

The Reverend A. J. Muste, with two companions, shakes hands with North Vietnamese leader Ho Chi Minh during a visit to that country to show support for its fight against the United States.

same as a lynch mob. The principle involved is taking the law into one's own hands."

All nine defendants said they acted to protest the Vietnam war. But Judge Roszell C. Thomasen said when he sentenced them that "none of us can have the freedom guaranteed us by the constitution unless people who disagree with the policy of the government express their disagreement by legal means rather than by violation of the law."

The defendants had stormed a draft board office in Catonsville, Maryland, seized the records, and burned them with homemade napalm. When they were arrested they became known on the New Left as the Catonsville Nine.

New Left activities in Chicago before and during the Democratic National Convention illustrate how demands were first made through legal channels, but once they were rejected the law was disregarded. An early statement by Tom Hayden of SDS laid open to question the sincerity of New Left attempts to negotiate with city officials. Hayden told an early planning meeting: "We should have people organized who can fight the police, who are willing to get arrested. No question that there will be a lot of arrests. My thinking is not to leave the initiative to the police. ...We don't want to get into the trap of violence versus passive action."

The first public moves by the New Left were made through legal channels. Rennie Davis, an SDS leader who also was an organizer for the National Mobilization Committee to End the War in Vietnam, negotiated with city officials in an effort to get permits for parades and the use of city parks. Davis willingly cooperated at this stage with Roger Wilkins, head of the Community Relations Service of the Department of Justice, who acted as an intermediary. Davis wanted permission for a demonstration near the convention hall.

"We wanted to have legal and undisrupted demonstrations," he said, "and we felt the real power of our coming to Chicago would be around those public hearings at the Amphitheatre, and that's really what we wanted to secure."

Also at issue was the use of parks. Davis wanted city permis-

Two of the Catonsville Nine, Father Philip Berrigan (left) and Father Daniel Berrigan, watch two baskets of draft board records burn.

sion for people having no other place to stay to sleep in the parks:

> If people come to Chicago with no place to go, and begin
> to sleep in parks, or wherever they can find a place to sleep,
> and then will be forced out of the park, that entirely breaks
> down our ability to provide organization, which leads to the
> kind of disruption that you and I both want to prevent, and
> the issue of peaceful assembly becomes shattered against a
> practical reality that people have no place to go and will be
> confronted by police, leading to disruption and possible violence
> all through the week of the convention.

Davis and the National Mobilization went to court to force
the city to grant the march permits it wanted as well as use of
the parks. The court rejected the petition. "Such a use of the
park," the judge ruled, "is in violation of existing ordinances,
and permits have never been granted for such a use in the past.
This court believes that it indeed would be a novel interpretation
to hold that the First and Fourteenth Amendments require a
municipal government to provide a public park as sleeping accommodations for persons desiring to visit the city."

From fruitless negotiations and courtroom arguments, the situation swiftly degenerated into bloody clashes in the streets once
the convention opened.

After the violence had started, the leftists could point to their
efforts to gain concessions from the city by legal means. This way,
it was hoped, the public would place some of the blame on un-
yielding city officials and, once again, a step would have been
taken toward undermining confidence in the fairness and justice
of our laws and the people who administer them.

Mob violence is an effective tactic for involving innocent
people and casting doubt on the actions of police and city officials.
The result can be an increasing timidity in enforcing the law.
Sanger points out where this can lead:

> Successful insurgency or revolt is habit forming. If rioters
> can get away with it in one place they will reason that they

Rennie Davis (left), an official of the National Mobilization Committee to End the War in Vietnam, confers with his lawyer during testimony before a special Senate subcommittee investigating demonstrations at the 1968 Democratic National Convention in Chicago.

can get away with it in ten more.

Perhaps some of our authorities are losing the courage to stick their necks out. This also is in the classic pattern, a sign of social disintegration.... It is of no value to a community to have a police chief who is fearful his police will be called brutal....

If policemen won't act, if the judges won't meet their responsibilities, if lawyers can keep their rioter-clients out of jail forever, if politicians are not willing to enact the required laws, you end up with an abdication of the will to govern.

The Communist Party and the New Left have similar attitudes toward the law. They consider American law to be a tool of the capitalist system, and they try, in a variety of ways, to turn it against that system.

Chapter Ten

Marxism: Food for the New Left

Today's world would shock Karl Marx. Socialism and communism haven't turned out to be as beneficial as he predicted. Capitalism has not only survived; it has shown a capacity for reform that Marx never thought possible. Instead of creating revolutionaries out of the working class, capitalism, especially in the United States, has produced the most prosperous workers the world has ever known.

But if today's world is not what Marx foresaw, that fact has not seemed to lessen the appeal of Marxism. What is the power of this doctrine to survive and attract new advocates with each succeeding generation? Why are American youth, growing up amid unprecedented prosperity in a capitalist society, looking to Marx for answers to the nation's problems?

There are two broad reasons for the lasting appeal of Marx: (1) he sympathized with the underdog, championed the lower classes; (2) he offered a simple explanation for the ills of the world —the villain was capitalism.

Today's world is far different from nineteenth century England and France that provided Marx with his view of capitalism and the problems he felt were its legacy. Even though some of the details may be different, the world still seeks cures for some of the same general ailments. There is still a great deal of poverty in the United

States and abroad. Nations still seek to resolve their differences through war.

And there is still capitalism to blame for the problems of the world.

Marx has a special appeal to the young and the have-nots of society. He does not tell people to work hard, be frugal, and someday you, too, can be rich and powerful. Instead he advocates a quick answer: revolution. The exploited members of society, says Marx, will rise up, take over society, and cast out the ruling classes who have refused to share their wealth and power. Marxism is a doctrine for the frustrated and the impatient. This accounts for much of its present-day appeal.

Why should the young people of the New Left be looking for answers anywhere but within the bountiful society existing in America? There are many reasons.

For some, it was the experience of working for voter registration in the deep South. They saw people kept from voting because of race. They also saw people beaten and churches bombed because they were part of a drive to register Negro voters.

For others it was the Vietnam war, a war they felt they would have to fight even though they doubted its justification.

For still others it was a society that seemed to be growing more and more impersonal, more machine-like.

And for many more, it was the fact that despite the impressive economic statistics of prosperity, there still was poverty in America.

For all these problems, Marx offered an answer: the fault was in the capitalist system. Under capitalism, said Marx, there had to be exploited classes, the Negro and the poor. The Vietnam war was easily explained by Marxism: an imperialist war, the inevitable capitalist drive for new markets and new sources for raw materials. A machine-like society? That was how Marx saw capitalism: a system that reduced labor to a means of production "devoid of every human characteristic of body and of spirit."

Marx called the working class the proletariat. He viewed the proletariat as dehumanized and exploited by capitalism. They were the downtrodden, the underdogs of society, and Marx rose eloquently to their defense. "In the fully developed proletariat," he wrote, "everything human, even a semblance of humanity is disregarded. . . . His existence, his life, becomes a supply of merchandise, like any other merchandise."

More than a century later, echoes of Marx's view could be found in the statement issued by the American students who met at Port Huron to found SDS. They wrote: "We regard men as infinitely precious and possessed of unfulfilled capacities for reason, freedom and love. In affirming these principles we are aware of countering perhaps the dominant conceptions of man in the Twentieth Century: that he is a thing to be manipulated, that he is inherently incapable of directing his own affairs. We oppose the depersonalization that reduces human beings to the status of things."

It is not just a few leaders of the New Left who feel this way. Professor Kenneth Keniston of Yale University spent the summer of 1967 interviewing young people who took part in Vietnam Summer, a New Left project designed to develop grass roots opposition to the war. Many of the views expressed by these young people echoed Marx's description of people stripped by society of "everything human, even a semblance of humanity."

One of the young people told of a job interview: "The person who was interviewing me said, 'This is a job that's open, this is what you must fit into.' That bothered me; it bothered me that I had to fit into this slot."

There are other close parallels between the writings of Marx a century ago and the statements of extreme leftists in America today. For example, on the subject of permanent revolution, Marx wrote:

> It is in our interest, and it is our duty to carry on permanent revolution until all of the more or less propertied classes have been driven from power, until the proletariat commands public power and until, not only in one land, but in all the principal lands of the world, the union of the proletariat will have made sufficient progress...to concentrate the essential means of production, at least, in the hands of the proletariat.

Milton Rosen, chairman of the Progressive Labor Party, wrote: "Only by destroying the political power of a small, greedy ruling class, can our people achieve their aspirations. By traveling the road to revolution, we will learn the strategy and tactics necessary to transfer political power to those who build and create the wealth and genius of our country."

Members of the extreme left repeat over and over their belief that meaningful change will come to American society only through revolution. And in saying so, they echo the belief of Friedrich Engels, close collaborator of Marx. It was Engels, son of a wealthy German capitalist, who wrote that "the revolution must come; it is already too late to find a solution to the problem."

One can even find parallels between the beliefs of the gun-toting, Mao-quoting Black Panthers and Marx who had said: "It is necessary to organize and arm the proletariat. The arming of the whole proletariat with rifles, guns and ammunition must be carried out at once."

Still another Marxist view that finds many adherents on the far left today is: "A people resolved to be independent should not be satisfied with conventional methods of warfare. Riots, revolt and guerrilla tactics are the ways by which a small nation can overcome a large one."

When rioting erupted in American cities, militants of the left such as Stokely Carmichael seemed to echo that view when they described the disorders as the start of "urban guerrilla warfare in the United States."

Do all leftists have the same view of Marx? Does Marxism mean the same thing to the Communist Party as it does to the New Left?

In their view of capitalism, both the New and Old Left accept the Marxist criticisms: the Negroes and the workers—whether they know it or not—are the exploited classes; the Vietnam war is an imperialist war being waged by the capitalist government of the United States.

Having identified the "devil," the various factions on the far left have differing interpretations of what the master teaches for dealing with him.

The Communist Party-U.S.A. has not abandoned violence and revolution as advocated by Marx and Engels, but the party has stopped calling the upheaval inevitable. The current party line

Karl Marx, father of the international communist movement.

Friedrich Engels, German socialist, who worked with Marx in developing the theory of modern-day communism.

calls violent revolution a last resort, to occur only if a majority of the population demands socialism and the government refuses to yield.

The young militants of the New Left stick closer to the classical Marxist view that the "ruling class" will never yield power willingly, and therefore violent revolution is inevitable.

Once a revolution takes place and the masses seize power, it is the Communist Party that would adhere to the economic doctrines of Marx. The current party line shies away from such extreme proposals as the abolition of private property or collective farming, but it would bring about the public takeover of major industries. There also would be, according to the party platform, a redistribution of wealth through "soak the rich" taxation. The party emphasizes that it is interested in establishing a peculiarly American brand of socialism in the United States. However, its consistent record of adherence to Soviet policy would indicate that its view of an ideal society would conform closely, if not exactly, to that of the Soviet Union.

The New Left looks elsewhere for Marxist models. While some New Leftists talk about socialism or communism as the answer for what they see as the ills of America, most are very vague about establishing a communist state. Their interest in Marx centers on what is wrong with capitalism and on his advocacy of revolution.

Communist China often is the nation New Leftists look to as a model. But even there, they show little interest in the structure of Chinese society and the changes brought about by Mao. To New Leftists, the most impressive event in China was the Cultural Revolution, which they viewed as an ultimate in democracy. This event, during which mobs of Red Guards roamed the streets denouncing, and in some cases holding impromptu trials of public officials, represented giving power to the people as opposed to the ever-present big governments of both the United States and the Soviet Union.

Critics of the New Left often cite the movement's preference for disorder. Author Leslie Fiedler, for example, calls members of the New Left the "new irrationalists" and "dropouts from history." New Leftists, says Fiedler, "deny all the apostles of reason,

Freud as well as Socrates; and if they seem to exempt Marx, this is because they know less about him, have heard him evoked less often by the teachers they are driven to deny."

The New Left gets its Marxism from men like C. Wright Mills, a huge Texan, who taught at Columbia University. A stinging critic of contemporary society, Mills, in the years just before his death, was a strong supporter of Fidel Castro. His best-known book was *The Power Elite.*

"On every hand," he wrote, "the individual is confronted with seemingly remote organizations; he feels dwarfed and helpless before the managerial cadres and their manipulated and manipulating minions."

In a passage with a particular appeal to the young students who make up the bulk of the New Left, Mills wrote: "Who is it that is getting fed up? Who is it that is getting disgusted with what Marx called the old crap? All over the world—in the [Soviet] bloc, outside the bloc and in between—the answer is the same: the young intelligentsia."

It is ironic that the leading hero of the young radicals, so mistrustful of their elders, is a mild-mannered philosopher in his seventies, Herbert Marcuse. Born in Germany, Marcuse was a founder of the Frankfurt Institute of Social Research, which was known for its Marxist approach to social problems.

Marcuse was one of those who fled the Nazis. He went first to Switzerland and then, in 1936, to the United States, where he became a lecturer at Columbia University. He became a U.S. citizen and during World War II served as a senior intelligence analyst for the Office of Strategic Services.

Generally condemned in the American press because of his Marxist philosophy and his rejection of the democratic process as a means of solving society's problems, Marcuse fares no better in the Soviet press. The Russians condemn him regularly as a counterrevolutionary influence on youth and often label him an agent of the U.S. Central Intelligence Agency.

Marcuse sees today's industrial society as irrational and restrictive. His view of individual freedom is one which casts off the restraints most people accept without question. Says Marcuse, "The realm of freedom is envisioned as lying beyond the realm of necessity: freedom is not within but outside the 'struggle for existence.' Possession and procurement of the necessities of life are the prerequisite, rather than the content, of a free society."

When students at Columbia University rebelled and paralyzed that school for weeks, Marcuse voiced his support of their demands. "My only disagreement would be on tactics," he said. "But after all, I am not a tactician. Nice separations between theory and tactics cannot always be made today, for after all, theory must have something to do with truth if it is to be in any way relevant to conditions."

Like so many of his disciples, Marcuse is not a proposer of alternatives to the system he criticizes: "I can't give anyone a blueprint of what that ideal society would or ought to be. When you get a truly free society, then people will be free to choose what sort of government they really want. No, it's not up to me to hand down a

Dr. Herbert Marcuse, professor at the University of California at San Diego, is a major source of New Left philosophy.

blueprint to them. That would be presumptuous."

A critical view of Marcuse is taken by Dr. Sidney Hook, professor of philosophy at New York University. Calling Marcuse muddle-headed, Hook gives this interpretation of the Marxist philosopher's view: "What he is saying is this: Democracy has failed because people choose things of which Marcuse disapproves. He is a Prussian type who believes that we should force people to be free, force them to love each other."

Most members of the New Left are not thinkers or philosophers. They are less inclined than their elders in the Old Left to split ideological hairs: they are activists.

One of their few claims to originality is the concept of "participatory democracy." It is an ill-defined concept that seems to reflect Marcuse's concern with the individual. It is, in effect, a rebellion against the bigness of universities, of businesses, of government, of all aspects of mid-twentieth century society. Under participatory democracy everyone would participate in all decision making. Under some interpretations, no decisions in the traditional sense are made. People simply respond as the spirit moves them.

As one member of SDS described the process, "Policies are set and action determined by those who in the maelstrom of discussion and debate exert the most influence through courage, articulateness, reasonableness and sensitivity to the feelings of the group. Influence is enhanced by image characteristics such as reputations, looks and style of living that appeal to young people."

This recollection by radical University of Chicago faculty member Staughton Lynd (formerly of Yale) gives another view of participatory democracy:

> Still more poignant was the perception—and I checked my reaction with many others who felt as I did—that as the crowd moved down the Mall towards the seat of government...so that there was nowhere to go but forward towards the waiting policemen, it seemed that the great mass of people would simply flow on through and over the marble building, that our forward movement [was] irresistibly strong, that had some been shot or arrested, nothing could have stopped that crowd from taking possession

of its government. Perhaps next time we should keep going.

To many New Left radicals, the classic instance of participatory democracy is the cultural revolution in Communist China. For many others, what the radical sees as participatory democracy seems to bear more similarity to anarchy.

There are two aspects to Marx's impact on the American far left.

The Communist Party, a traditional Marxist party, accepts Marx's view of capitalism and his economic theories. However, Lenin and other Soviet leaders have discarded some of Marx's doctrines and drastically altered others. For the Communist Party-U.S.A., the Marxist road to follow is the one prescribed by the Soviet Union.

To members of the New Left, Marxism provides a doctrine that expresses their feelings of frustration and discontent with the American system. Marx agrees with their list of the ills of society and tells them capitalism is the cause. And he offers a solution: revolution.

Chapter Eleven

The Outlook for the Left

During the past five years, Americans have watched the extreme left revive and then expand in a spectacular way. They have heard speakers again and again call for the overthrow of capitalism, for a Marxist-Leninist revolution in the United States. They have seen campuses disrupted and cities ablaze. And many wonder whether the extreme left is approaching its principal goal, whether revolution is getting under way in America.

What does the future hold for the Communist Party-U.S.A. and the New Left? Are they actually moving closer to the goals they have set? Will they continue to grow until the Communist Party becomes a factor in American elections and the New Left holds a veto power over the operations of universities? How does the government plan to deal with the extreme left?

It is impossible to answer these questions with certainty, but there are some signs that can be examined for clues to the future.

To get some idea of whether the extreme left will continue to thrive, we might review the issues which led to its revival. They include:

• The Vietnam war. The war overshadows all other issues as a factor in the growth of the far left. Had there been no Vietnam war, it seems highly unlikely that the Far Left would have grown nearly as much as it did.

• The early civil rights campaigns. It was on these campaigns in the deep South that many young Americans decided there was something very wrong with America. They saw authority used to suppress what they believed were legitimate attempts to correct long-standing grievances. They saw people beaten and killed because they were trying to arouse people to register and vote.

• The problems of Negro ghettoes. The vast, teeming Negro slums in our major cities present a new array of problems to all levels of government. Few if any have been solved.

• University life. Students became increasingly aware of and increasingly distressed by the impersonality of America's large universities and by seeming unwillingness to become involved in the communities around them.

• Loss of confidence in government. The far left and the far right come together in their determination to look outside government for answers to the problems of society.

If the Vietnam war ends and if the nation avoids becoming entangled in similar wars in Asia, the far left will have lost its biggest issue. It will have lost the one issue on which it was able to work with and be accepted by people outside the left.

Ironically, if the United States arrives at a settlement in Vietnam and withdraws, the far left will be able to claim a victory. And that victory might destroy its reason for existence.

The forays by idealistic students into Mississippi and other states of the deep South in the early 1960s have ended. Southern Negroes in ever greater numbers are asserting their right to vote as evidenced by the rapidly growing numbers of Negro elected officials in the deep South. Thus, one other major issue that drove many young people leftward no longer exists.

It has been replaced by racial problems in big cities. Federal officials point out that major cities have avoided riots since the wave that swept the nation in the summer of 1967 with the exception of the rioting that followed the assassination of Dr. Martin Luther King, Jr., in the spring of 1968. However, they add, while large-scale rioting may not occur again, racial tension remains high. The fear among many officials at all levels of government

Harlem, one of the largest concentrations of blacks in the United States, located on the island of Manhattan in New York City, offers extremists countless opportunities for igniting violence and trouble.

Captain R. J. Ranney halts two Black Panthers as they march up the steps of the state capitol building at Olympia, Washington, with loaded rifles. He ordered them to unload the guns, and they complied.

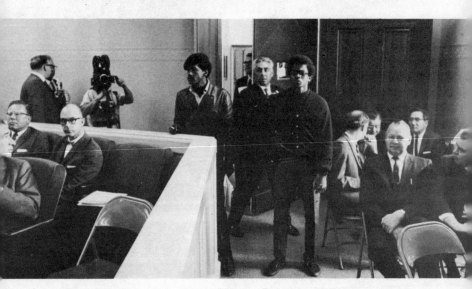

Two members of the Black Panther Party, carrying arms, appear in the Assembly chamber at Sacramento, California, to protest a bill before the Legislature which would restrict the carrying of arms in public.

is that tension may break out into sporadic cases of terrorism or the sort of urban guerrilla warfare advocated by extremists of the left.

Universities remain potentially explosive. SDS is split into two warring factions. Whether that split will make each faction more militant or will dilute the organization's effectiveness remains to be seen. Many universities have moved to meet some of the student demands. To the militants this only means that other demands must be presented to continue the confrontation with authority. The question remains of whether the majority on campuses will support further demands.

Many who turn to the far left are searching for what they hope will be new ways to solve the problems of our society. They feel that solutions advocated by the administration in power will not work. The feeling extends beyond the far left. Those who turn to the extremes of either right or left reject the solutions of the two major parties in the United States. They say that they see little difference between them. While many people express a lack of confidence in old solutions, few seem ready to turn to the extreme answers of either the New or Old Left.

What has all the noise and agitation on the left meant to the Communist Party? The party is undoubtedly stronger today than it was five years ago. It is back in the open, no longer threatened by government action. But it now faces a new threat, this one from the left.

The New Left, Black Power, and Czechoslovakia are all creating problems for the party.

Visit the room of a young militant member of SDS and you are likely to find a poster with a picture of Mao or Castro or Che Guevara. They are the heroes of the New Left. There are no posters with pictures of Leonid Brezhnev or Alexei Kosygin. Most New Leftists view the Soviet leadership as similar to the American. The Russian revolution often is described by New Leftists as having been "captured by the bureaucracy."

The party also has had problems dealing with militant blacks. J. Edgar Hoover described the party in early 1969 as—

confronted with the dilemma of losing hold and influence over
the more militant Negro youth within the party because of the
attractiveness of the reckless propaganda of black power advocates. . . . The Communist Party-U.S.A. claims to disagree
with these extreme positions at this particular time but conciliates them for fear of being isolated from this sector of youth.
It conciliates so much, in fact, that it is hard to determine
whether the Communist Party is really for or against Black
Power.

The Soviet invasion of Czechoslovakia in August 1968 split the
party internally and tarnished its image before the general public.
The party met in New York less than a month after the invasion
and adopted by a reported one-vote margin a resolution censuring
leaders who deviated from the Moscow line. Mike Stein, executive secretary of the New York district, called the motion "vin-
dictive." Gilbert Green, chairman of the New York district, called
the Czech invasion "a very serious blunder."

In addition to these problems, the party faces the threat of
being eclipsed by the New Left. It is the New Left that is in the
vanguard of protests throughout the country. And it is the New
Left that is likely to be the object of any government crackdown
on the extreme left.

The administration of President Lyndon B. Johnson seemed at
times beseiged by protestors. It wasn't long after he succeeded
Johnson that President Nixon voiced some of the impatience felt
by many Americans with campus radicals. The President referred
to their "self-righteous moral arrogance" and said it "denies the
most fundamental of all values we hold: respect for the rights of
others. . . .

"The student who invades an administration building, roughs
up the dean, rifles the files and issues 'non-negotiable demands'
may have some of his demands met by a permissive university
administration. But the greater his 'victory' the more he will
have undermined the security of his own rights."

Both the President and his attorney general, John N. Mitchell,
called upon college administrators to crack down more swiftly

than in the past on lawless demonstrations. "When police authority is needed to restore law and order, the courts or the local police should be utilized immediately," Mitchell told a House committee.

He also outlined what the Justice Department is doing to help in a crackdown on the extremists in the New Left. Federal investigators, particularly from the FBI, are being used, Mitchell said, to collect information on the disorders and those who cause them. Much of the information is passed on to local authorities while the Justice Department also is checking to see if some individuals are liable to prosecution under existing federal laws.

The possibility of punitive action by Congress is disturbing many college administrators. The House Education and Labor Committee struggled for weeks to come up with a moderate bill dealing with campus disorders. It failed. Cause of the controversy was a section that would have cut off federal aid to colleges that failed to adopt codes of student conduct. It was killed in committee, leaving as the only punitive section the provision cutting off aid to individual students who participate in disruptive campus demonstrations.

The fear was not that a weak bill would pass, but that if the committee could not write a moderate bill, far harsher penalties would be offered as amendments from the House floor. One such provision would make it a federal crime, punishable by three years in prison and a $5,000 fine, to commit any act of violence, enter a college building, or block access to it with intent to interfere with operation of the college.

Administration officials, including Robert Finch, secretary of health, education, and welfare, and Dr. James Allen, commissioner of education, opposed any new legislation. The same is true of most college administrators.

Nathan M. Pusey, president of Harvard University, testified before the House committee a month after his school had been disrupted for days by an SDS-led demonstration. He pleaded with House members "not to seek to effect correction by hasty enactments which cannot reach to the root of the difficulty and will, in all probability, only spread the discontent."

Asked what assurance he could offer that he could deal with

rebellious students, Pusey said, "I think we can do it. We have got to get rid of a small group of revolutionaries and then work with the other students."

But Representative William D. Hathaway of Maine, who graduated from Harvard in 1949, told Pusey: "It would be difficult to persuade more than 40 or 50 members of the House to agree to place a moratorium" on enactment of legislation dealing with campus disorders. Within Harvard there was little agreement over Pusey's handling of the SDS disorders, particularly his summoning of local police to clear an occupied building. A student-faculty report criticized the administration, saying that "the policy chosen showed firmness but little imagination and not enough trust."

Tough legislation by Congress, of course, will oblige college officials to crack down hard on the New Left.

Developments in general tend to move toward some of the pessimistic prophecies at recent graduation ceremonies. For example, John W. Gardner, former secretary of health, education, and welfare, told an audience at Stanford University: "The student with an inclination toward violent or coercive action and the policeman with a taste for brutality are waiting for each other."

"A year ago," Gardner recalled, "a young acquaintance of mine confidently said, 'The universities can be destroyed,' and I laughed at him. I laugh no longer."

When the radical and the policeman meet in bloody battle, the result has not yet been a suppression of radicalism. On the contrary, the New Left seems to have thrived on such clashes.

Michael A. Bernstein, top-ranking scholar in the Princeton University 1969 graduating class, told his fellow graduates that the United States was "sick." He based his diagnosis, he said, on the fact the country "uses helicopters and guns on our brothers in Berkeley, Missouri, and Vietnam.

"More, perhaps, than ever before, we realize as a class," said Bernstein, "that what happens to the Panthers in New York, the Presidio 17, or the strikers at Mahwah is intimately linked to our destinies, that their options open up possibilities for us, and that their defeat would be ours as well."

With the New Left gaining support among students and with

Congress becoming increasingly impatient with campus violence, college administrators find themselves caught in a vise. The split in the ranks of SDS could add to the pressure. SDS regulars and Progressive Laborites could become even more militant in their efforts to win new support. It is a prospect that worries many college administrators.

In its statement on campus disorders, the National Commission on Violence singled out the stand of Kingman Brewster, president of Yale, as one that others might well follow.

Brewster's policy states:

Proposition one is the encouragement of controversy, no mat-

Police battle student demonstrators at the University of Connecticut during protest of on-campus recruitment by the Olin-Mathieson Corporation. Groups like the SDS promote such dramatic confrontations as a means of "radicalizing" otherwise neutral students.

ter how fundamental; and the protection of dissent, no matter how extreme. This is not just to permit the "letting off of steam" but because it will improve [the university] as a place to be educated.

Proposition number two is a convincing intention to deal speedily and firmly with any forcible interference with student and faculty activities or the normal use of any [university] facilities. . . . I see no basis for compromise on the basic proposition that forcible coercion and violent intimidation are unacceptable means of persuasion and unacceptable techniques of change in a university community, as long as channels of communication and the chance for reasoned arguments are available.

Amid the chaos often generated by SDS, how many administrators will be able to apply Brewster's propositions? Will more frequent summons of police restore order on campuses or swell the ranks of radicals? Past experience indicates the latter.

To many students, police on campus fit this description which Tom Hayden gave the Violence Commission:

Working in the South [on civil rights] brought us face to face for the first time with the reality that we had never known, the direct reality of the police state. . . . The crucial discovery of that experience for many students, however, was that the South was not an isolated and backward region but was an integral part of the whole country. . . .

An elementary lesson began to dawn on us, a lesson that never was taught us in our civics classes, and that lesson was simply that law serves power.

However, not all the signs and prophecies are gloomy. At Harvard's graduation, a member of SDS was given time to speak. When he began by denouncing the university, he was booed and hooted by the audience. Moments later another student speaker was cheered when he chided the administration for having "broken the best heads in the country, embittered the most creative minds and turned off their most talented scholars."

John Kenneth Galbraith, Harvard economist and author, told a commencement audience at Massachusetts Institute of Technology: "I am struck by the gloom that pervades the modern university community. . . . I do not wish to seem an optimist. I am not above protecting my reputation for scholarship and insight by spreading a little gloom. But let us not be too depressed. Universities are going to survive."

Two factors that will go a long way toward determining whether they survive in peace or chaos are the split in the SDS and the course of the war in Vietnam.

All the radicalism and all the Marxist theory are unlikely to sustain campus rebellion at the level of the past few years if the war ends. Continued de-escalation of the war would remove the major issue that the New Left has had. If the war ends, so will draft protests. So too will much of the opposition to ROTC and defense research.

The New Left is not likely to collapse with the end of the war, but its gut issue will be gone. It will then be up to movement leaders to try to arouse young people over unsolved domestic problems such as poverty and racial discrimination. A new target is certain to be the conservative cast of the Nixon administration.

Where has the unrest led so far? Where have the greatest changes occurred?

The antiwar movement, denounced at first from the White House and Capitol Hill alike, expanded and attracted millions of supporters, producing a shift in government policy.

Campus unrest brought many fundamental changes. Students gained a new voice in the decision making at many universities. At Princeton, for example, a black graduate who had taken part in demonstrations against university investments in South Africa was named to the board of trustees. Black studies programs also have won acceptance at many universities despite opposition from conservative civil rights leaders.

New Left protests forced changes in ROTC and defense research at some schools.

Some of the accomplishments of the New Left are now being overshadowed by divisions within the movement. In addition to the split in the SDS, there is the fight among some academic radicals over demands for black studies programs.

The split over black studies was aired by Professor Eugene D. Genovese, former history professor at Rutgers University in New Jersey. Genovese's vehement opposition to U.S. policy in Vietnam while he was teaching at the state-supported school made him an issue in the 1965 New Jersey gubernatorial campaign.

Recently, in an article in the *Atlantic*, Genovese criticized university administrators for "a cowardly surrender" to student demands. He blamed "pseudo-revolutionary totalitarians within the left-wing student movement" who, he said, "are inflaming the black studies issue in the hope of provoking political purges in the

Members of the Black Panther Party stage a silent demonstration outside a court building in New York City to protest indictment of 21 party members accused of plotting violence and terror.

faculties." Their tactics, he concluded, will "provide a moral and legal basis for a new wave of McCarthyism."

In the area of race relations, black militants of the New Left such as Stokely Carmichael shifted emphasis from integration to revolution through violence and black power. However, Carmichael is in exile and those who remained at home to mind the Black Panthers no longer see eye to eye with him.

Carmichael unexpectedly broke with the Black Panther Party and resigned as a result of differences over a decision to form alliances with white radicals.

In a letter explaining his action, Carmichael wrote: "The alliances being formed by the party are alliances which I cannot politically agree with, because the history of Africans living in the United States has shown that any premature alliance with white radicals has led to complete subversion of the blacks by the whites through their direct or indirect control of the black organization."

Carmichael also accused the Panther Party of becoming "dogmatic in its newly acquired ideology [Marxism]. . . . All those who disagree with the party line, in part or completely, are lumped into the same category and labeled cultural nationalists, reactionary pigs, etc."

David Hilliard, Panther chief of staff, commented that Carmichael "just did not come to understand that you can't fight racism with racism. . . . It doesn't matter if you are black, white or brown. The enemy is capitalism and racism. You can only get rid of them by practicing solidarity, not more racism."

This new position of the Black Panthers may reopen the door to a coalition between extremist blacks and extremist whites, a coalition to which the "white" as well as the "yellow" communists might be admitted.

However, such a coalition, based on the principle of revolution and rejecting the principle of integration, can hardly hope to attract the mass of black Americans. The latter want a bigger piece of the pie, to which they undoubtedly are entitled. And they must know, consciously or unconsciously, that neither the black nor the white extremists are in a position to give this to them. If they are to get it, it must come from those who have it to give—

the established society as it now exists under the Constitution of the United States.

The dominant elements of this society already have embarked on a course intended to integrate black citizens on a basis of equality with whites. This is the course advocated by moderate black leaders. It would seem that the coalition of moderate whites and blacks has better prospects of growth than that of the extremist whites and blacks.

The main achievement of the extremists may turn out to be the cementing of the coalition between the moderates and the speeding up of the integration of blacks into the predominantly white society of the United States.

The effect of the antiwar demonstrations could be to hasten the end of the conflict in Vietnam.

Agitation on the campus already has produced university reforms as demanded by both white and black students.

Taken together, these developments in the direction of peace, a better deal for blacks, and a better deal for students should have the effect of destroying the roots of both communism and the New Left and eliminating them as a threat to the constitutional system of the United States.

Appendix

DOCUMENT No. 1

Black Panther Objectives

From the Political Education Kit for Black Panther Party Members, exhibited at Hearings before the Permanent Subcommittee on Investigations of the Senate Committee on Government Operations, June 18, 24, and 25, 1969.

Primary Objective of Our Party: To establish Revolutionary Political Power for Black People.

The Black Panther is an armed body for carrying out the political tasks of the revolution. Especially at the present, the Black Panther Party should certainly not confine itself to only fighting; besides fighting to destroy the enemy's military strength, our Party must also shoulder such important tasks as doing propaganda among the masses, organizing the masses, arming Black people, helping them to establish revolutionary political power and setting up party organizations. The Black Panther Party defends itself with guns and force not merely for the sake of fighting but in order to conduct propaganda among the masses, organize them, arm them, and help them to establish revolutionary political power. Without these objectives, fighting loses its meaning and the Black Panther Party loses the reason for its existence.

CARDINAL RULE: Have Faith in the People and Faith in the Party.

DOCUMENT No. 2

How to Conduct Urban Warfare

From a Black Panther pamphlet, listed as Exhibit No. 629 in Hearings before the Permanent Subcommittee on Investigations of the Senate Committee on Government Operations, June 26 and 30, 1969.

URBAN WARFARE: DUTY

As we shall now see in the northern areas of this country the problem is not so much how to isolate the big cities but instead how to attack the system inside of these cities. You see the bulk of the population live in the cities which is where the majority of the people work. In other parts of the country one can easily see that the reverse is the case. We must also keep in mind that a overall strategy would include simultaneous ATTACKS on suburban areas and urban areas, but this will be covered later on.

Let us take a city called Delta, which might have a population of say 8 million people. You must take many things into consideration before you attempt to carry thru with your plan. (1) At what time is this city most congested at a given point? (2) What is the location of all state and city barracks? (3) What is the location of all fire and civil defense units? (4) Can you get a complete map of streets, traffic directions and hospitals? (5) Do you have a map containing the location of transportation lines, gas and water lines? (6) What is the attitude of the people in the city? How would they react during and after the ATTACK. This is very important because it sets the stage which your propaganda unit can take advantage of. By use of pamphlets, notices, wall posters, the public can be controlled and conditioned to accept whatever you want it to accept. (7) With the known situation above you can then proceed to select ATTACK teams and weapons to be carried by each team for the ATTACK.

Your particular mission might call for the use of wire cutters, electrical gloves, or small detonation devices, and the other teams might call for light or heavy automatic weapons, molotov fire bombs, rifles with scopes. All of this must be planned in advance the same way you would proceed to play a game of football, each man having a specific job and a specific time to do it. (in later chapter we will cover the actual weapons in their entirety and the basic team tactics) (8) Now the plan of ATTACK can be drawn up. This will be drawn up to the smallest detail. Practice missions should be run so as to make sure each member of the ATTACK and supporting teams knows his job. Experience has shown that simplicity is the key to an operation. The simpliar the plan the more efficiently it can be pulled off. This is by no means to imply that chances can't be taken. Sound tactics and simplicity will strike terror into the hearts of the enemy. In setting up an ATTACK the GUERRILLA must realize one important aim, the destruction of his target. Be it man, building, electro plant, train, what have you. The destruction of this target is of prime importance for many reasons. First of all the psychological effect of destroying the enemies complex within his own area will be devastating. The enemy will start to second guess himself. He will start to double check his security if not just increase it. And finally he will make that fatal mistake of becoming more rigid. The Imperalist getting rigid in his own mechanical society is something that will aid the GUERRILLA.

This is already a complex society, so you can imagine what will happen to the system when one bolt is destroyed in a factory and everything comes to a grinding halt. When one highway intersection is destroyed, vehicles coming from four or six directions come to a halt. When one traffic light is tripped every other traffic light in that area becomes messed up. Yes indeed the enemy will try to repair it as soon as possible. But while he is repairing one target the GUERRILLA has struck at another and another and still another point. Thus we come to the second rule for you the GUERRILLA: The enemy must be KEPT OFF BALANCE in the beginning stages. The enemy will always be able to muster troops to one point and another. But that takes time. Therefore he cannot be where the GUERRILLA is at the same time as the GUERRILLA because you will maintain the initiative. This is maintained by constant ATTACKS AT varied spots in the city. You will employ AMBUSH on AMBUSH. This means that an ATTACK on a avenue that the enemy is known to use will just be a trick to get him to stop and attack you. Once he has stopped he exposes himself to the main AMBUSH which is meant to destroy his (enemies) vehicles (troop carriers, tanks, police cars). This then leaves the GUERRILLA free to ATTACK with his other teams in another area of the city and destroy other targets. YOU see in this case the AMBUSH on AMBUSH WAS USED to make the enemy think that this was the main ATTACK when actually it was just a device to delay him and at the same time expose him to possible destruction. This leaves the main team to ATTACK in full force at another target and thereby complete the mission of the day.

Brothers, these tactics are not games; they are being used today in cities where the people are ATTACKING the system. You must no longer play, but plan. These tactics, these different missions cannot succeed to any degree unless they are planned and even more, practiced. In your ATTACK each team, each member of a team must know his job inside out. The liberation of our people depends on it.

Reviewing the above, let us look once more at the necessity of planning your missions down to the smallest detail. This also includes one or all of the above items. Timing: who will be where at what time, to do what job? How long will it take the enemy to react from his barracks or police stations? What will be the enemies most likely route to our target, and how will we delay him? How many and what type weapons will we use, and for what purpose? And last but not least, what will be reaction of our people to this ATTACK and how will the enemy be destroyed by this action?

REMEMBER THE BLACK GUERRILLA IS TRULY LIKE A MATCH STICK IN A BARN FULL OF HAY. IT IS UP TO US IF WE WANT TO BURN THE BARN DOWN.

WEAPONS, FIRE BOMB

I) The Guerrilla in the city is essentially a "street fighter". His main aim is to surprise the enemy, hit him where he is weakest, and to vanish into the cities maze of buildings, cellars and alley ways. His defense will be surprise, his weapon will be his ability to create new types of ambush. Therefore the arms that this type of GUERRILLA carries will have to be adapted to the physical structure of the city.

(a) Concrete and asphalt are a city's trade mark; sharp corners and narrow streets are also trade marks. Ready made sewage systems, basements and rooftops are also trade marks of the city, and the GUERRILLA who fights in this environment will have to take all of these into account. You the GUERRILLA must recognize the difference between warfare in the city and that outside of the city, for one might have to bury "cache" or supplies. These supply depots will have to be under ground and situated so that they are within reasonable traveling distance. The city is different. It is the accumulation of wealth and goods of an entire state or country. Therefore you must look at the city as cockroach looks at a food closet which he is inside of; all it takes is the ability to adapt and take what you need.

Now, fire is a prime weapon of the GUERRILLA in the city. With fire he cause the significant and insignificant building, store, car, etc. to become targets because of their direct relationship to things around them or close by. A fire will spread and cause much damage to the peace and tranquility of a given area. It will call the police and fire department (and in times of attack the national guard) to its area. This means that there will be some confusion when these fires are started in different areas.

The ability to fight man made fires is limited in city areas. It will become harder when the GUERRILLA uses them in a systematic manner. Fires can be used to sucker police and fire units into a particular area where upon they can be attacked by you the GUERRILLA. And if by chance the enemy should decide to guard his fire equipment with police or army troops, we the GUERRILLA will immediately put them under *automatic fire*. This becomes a problem for the enemy. Because he cannot protect all of his fire equipment with police or national guard detachments for they are needed to fight or rather try to combat the GUERRILLA.

Now fire is a weapon that can be very powerful when used in the proper manner. It can be used in areas where there is a cluster of buildings which contain inflammable substances. An example would be the garment district of any particular city or an area that has a number of warehouses. Gas lines are another prime target. Under the city run electrical water and gas lines. A sudden electrical fire can close down the working of a large section of a city. The starting of a fire near water lines can burn away tubing and thus cause an excessive amount of water to start collecting in the sewerage system.

Gas lines present the most exclusive target in the area. For this you need a map which contains the layout of gas lines throughout the city. Also remember must buildings today use oil as fuel and that also present another target.

Now Molotov fire bombs can be used for all the above targets mentioned. Furthermore the fire bomb can be made, carried, and even, in some cases, even thrown without anyone noticing. Basically it is a bottle containing a flammable liquid or solid with a rag sticking out of the neck which will be lit just before throwing or . . . it at the target. If the target happens to be in an area containing a high amount of fuel or other inflammable substances, you will probably have to devise some type of fuse. This is done so that you will also have some time to make good your escape. Now fire bombs can also be used against people as shock treatment. For example, whereever there is a crowd of people, there is the potential of panic. In some cities five o'clock or five thirty in the evening is the rush hour. It is also the hour of mass hysteria. It is the time of the day when people are usually tired and hot. It is at times like this that that anything can trigger their sense of fear and panic. These people are accustomed to train stoppages and things like this, but they are not used to anything frightening or which may threaten their lives. This is the time when the GUERRILLA must strike. And if he chooses fire as his weapon, he must also KILL or CRIPPLE as many of the enemy as possible. For only this will leave the rest psyschologically in a state of fear. The confusion will hamper the efforts of the police or guard to help them. In fact it probably will add to the confusion.

Now in a crowd like this one must make his fire bomb with a lot of petroleum. This will give the fire a napalm effect and thereby stick to the skin and clothes of the enemy. When others in the confusion see the effect of this type of ATTACK they will think of nothing but running and running, trampling each other and causing more injury and confusion. Now the most obvious question is how to accomplish this without being spotted by the enemy. First of all, as a GUERRILLA your duties will always include danger. But danger is the blood in the GUERRILLAS body. He lives with it and accepts it as a part of life. With this understanding we can see also that teamwork is needed in every mission. Effective teamwork will make the GUERRILLA team more dangerous. In a crowd, diversion is the key. People are curious by nature, so that an incident in one corner of a station will draw everyone's attention in that direction, leaving the other part of the team to set their charges and disappear. In missions like this a practice run or runs should be made to insure perfect results. These practice runs can be made either in the target area or in another area similar to your target.

DOCUMENT No. 3

Message from Mao Tse-tung

The November 1968 issue of the *Crusader*, monthly newsletter of the Republic of New Africa movement, was published in Peking while its leader, Robert F. Williams, was living there in exile prior to his return to the United States to answer charges of kidnapping. The issue, exhibited during the June 1969 Hearings before the Permanent Subcommittee on Investigations of the Senate Committee on Government Operations, included the following message:

I call on the workers, peasants and revolutionary intellectuals of every country and all who are willing to fight against U.S. imperialism to take action and extend strong support to the struggle of the black people in the United States! People of the whole world, unite still more closely and launch a sustained and vigorous offensive against our common enemy, U.S. imperialism, and against its lapse of colonialism, imperialism and all systems of exploitation, and the complete emancipation of all the oppressed peoples and nations of the world are not far off.

Mao Tse-tung

Work-In Manual for SDS Organizers

Exhibited at Hearings before the Permanent Subcommittee on
Investigations of the Senate Committee on Government Operations, June 16 and 17, 1969.

THE WORK-IN ORGANIZERS MANUAL

This manual is intended to help WORK-IN organizers in selecting and
getting jobs. It also contains some pointers on approaches to the political
issues that we will be raising and encountering at work.

I. HOW TO RESEARCH THE JOB SITUATION IN YOUR AREA

In every large city and in all states, a Directory of Manufacturers is
published which lists all the manufacturing plants in the large metropolitan areas and in the state, city by city. It usually reports the number
of workers employed in each plant and sometimes gives the breakdown
of male and female workers. These directories are usually found in the
main (large) city libraries.

These books usually cover only manufacturing. For transportation
(railroad, maritime, longshore, airline, teamster) possibly the simplest
method is to consult the yellow pages of the phone directory, although
there may be additional directories in the library. Consult the librarian
about that. This is also true for utilities, etc.

In addition, some people will already know of large plants in their
area in which they or friends have worked in the past, which might be
helpful since knowledge of hiring practices might be gained thereby.

II. WHAT JOBS TO LOOK FOR

Job-seekers should try to get hired in plants or transport depots that
have several hundred (let's say a 400 minimum) workers. Reasons for
this include: (a) If we want to reach workers with literature, the potential
audience is greater; (b) The larger the company facility, the better chance
that it will be in a basic union, that the workers will have some sense
of organization (even if they think the union is a sellout one), and that
therefore there will be a tie-in to workers nationally. In larger plants,
such as GM, GE, United Airlines, Pennsy RR, etc., there is a greater

tendency for workers to regard themselves as workers, with less illusions about becoming some kind of a "boss". In small shops, where bosses and workers are closer together, more illusions exist about "moving up". (c) In large plants in national unions there is a greater chance that the workers will become part of (and have a history of) mass strike movements, rebellions against sellout leaderships, conflict with the government due to "national interest" injections, etc., which might create the basis for greater mutual exchange about questions relating to opposition to the government's policies; (d) the larger the company the likelier the existence of masses of unskilled jobs (assembly lines, platforms, etc.) creating a better basis for hiring especially as replacements for workers taking vacations. Of course, if summer is slack in a particular industry, this situation wouldn't necessarily hold (i.e., auto, where production on the old model fades into a summer lay-off changeover before hiring starts around August to September for the new model).

Within the larger plant situation, it might be desirable for students seeking jobs in the area or city in which their school is located, to pick a place which would have follow-up possibilities in the Fall through contacts established within the plant, in line with an on-going worker-student alliance activity.

In general, people should seek unskilled jobs (probably couldn't get a skilled one anyway) and, if given the choice, a job where one would contact larger numbers of workers. If you are white, select a plant where the majority are white. (If possible. In some places, for instance, N.Y.C., this is difficult, although not impossible). While Black workers might be thought of as more politically conscious, what we as white students are trying to do is reach white workers on the questions of the war and racism, to name but two areas (in addition to the day-to-day grievances, trade union questions, etc.) If Black, a student would of necessity, have to (and should) get a job where there are large numbers of Black workers. Women should give special consideration to jobs where many women are employed. These include, in addition to basic industries (like electric) department stores, telephone companies, hospitals, and even some large offices which are unionized, etc.

In cases where people cannot travel to (or don't want to get jobs in) auto industries, large wholesale and retail outfits within the city proper could be as advantageous—large mail-order houses (Sears-Roebuck, Montgomery Ward department stores, preferably those with unions); possibly as non-professional workers in hospitals (although here in many large cities there are large majorities of Black workers, a factor for white students to consider.) Other such places could include the telephone company, gas and light company, mass utilities (if privately owned; government-owned usually requires a civil service test and waiting period).

III. HOW TO GET A JOB

Some places hire students specifically for the summer as replacements for workers on vacations (although usually bosses try to get away with not filling in, unless the union contract has specific stipulations and they are enforced). Others won't hire you if they know you are a student or if they think you're only working for the summer. In MOST cases it would probably be best NOT to mention that you are a student (unless you have advance knowledge that they are specifically hiring students for the summer—which might be found out by someone being sent there first who's NOT looking for a job, saying he's a student and seeing if they are hiring). If, then, it is the case of not being able to state you're a student seeking summer work, you have to come in as a job-seeker who has worked since graduating high-school (you should say you're a high school graduate), which means you have to have a place or person who will say you worked there for the past 1–4 years. Each area should develop "background" like this for their group. In indicating the kind of work performed, try to slant it to what you presume the work is in the particular plant or depot (assembly, maintenance, shipping, loading platform, etc., and in most every case indicate that whatever you did on your "previous job" involved some kind of manual, heavy work. You're not afraid to work, is the idea to get across.

If getting to the place requires a car (or if that is easier even though you use public transportation) say you have one or a friend who works around there, drives near there every day. Some places won't hire you if they think that you are potential late-comer.

Draft status may be a problem. Job applicants with a 1-Y or even 4-F often find difficulty in getting work. Also, a 2-S classification immediately identifies you as a student. Persons with a 3-A deferment (supporting a parent or child) have an easier time. If you're a 1-A (and possibly someone's tested the draft situation at the place beforehand), you might be able to say you're 1-A and get hired, but here again you may have to "use your wits". If you've been in and had an honorable discharge, tell it the way it is. If you've had something other than an honorable discharge, avoid mentioning it; you've been "working since high school."

In cases where you can't mention college, and use a "background" make sure you state you were "laid off" from your last job because it was "slow" or the company's "contracting" or maybe even "going out of business". Whatever salary you decide on (usually around $85/week —that is, not too much lower than what you expect to make, and not too much higher) make sure that your "former boss" knows what it is. For example, if you're going for a teamster platform job that pays $110 or $120 a week, say you make about $100, not $75. On the other hand, if you're getting a job in a hospital or a department store for $65 a week, say you made that figure in your old job, not $120. Anyway, since most large places will or may (unless you're specifically being hired as a temporary worker who's going back to college in the Fall), make sure your former boss has the story straight.

Some places give aptitude tests. Don't show off. If you're taking the test with other job-seekers, try to see how far (number of questions) they're getting and adjust accordingly. If you do too well, they'll either be suspicious or want to use you in the "front office." Of course, it may be hard to judge, not wanting to do below what's required, but again, the first job-seeker's experience will be helpful here. A group should gather ALL information from each successive job-seeker so that the next ones will be better prepared.

If you have any physical defects which can't be detected from a normal physical examination, don't mention them. Companies won't hire people with previous injuries or defects which might be re-injured, creating the basis for suits against them, they are very wary on this score. If it's a defect that's noticeable, either play it up to figure a way to cover it up. If you can't you may have to go somewhere else where it's not so important. If you wear glasses, some jobs are out (i.e. railroad brakeman, which usually requires 20/20 vision without glasses). However, most jobs only require 20/20 or even less with glasses.

You should be at your first place looking at around 8:30 or 9:00 A.M. It's hard to get a job if you start at 2:00 P.M. You generally should not wear a suit and tie or fancy dress, but DON'T dress like a slob. Slacks and sports shirt, with or without a sport jacket, depending on the weather, and skirt or summer dress with low heels (or at least not 6-inch spikes) for women.

If places require a "non-communist" or "non-subversive" signature, sign it. You're not breaking any law. If it's engaged in government work, and you would be breaking a law, it will be so stated on the application. Discuss this beforehand with your group.

Be straightforward in any interview; you're getting the job because you "need the money." Don't use $20 words. Don't put on a tough guy act. Just plain, simple language and attitude. Usually the less said, the better. Don't volunteer information. Just answer what is asked.

IV. WHAT TO EXPECT ON THE JOB

Don't start sounding off the first day on the job; or even the first week. Do your work, learn your job. Don't goof off on someone else's back, but if all the workers are goofing off, or taking a break, go ahead (unless it might cost you—as a new worker—your job, which the older workers understand). Remember, we're here for a short-term operation. While you can't expect to win over workers in three months, you don't have to wait as long as you might, if it were a permanent job, to "open up" on political questions. LEARN FROM THE WORKERS. About the work, the job, the history of the plant, company, union, their attitudes on every question. Listen. You might find out who the finks are. Participate in the bull sessions, the lunch discussions, talking on the job where it's normal, but take it slow the first 3 or 4 weeks, (if the job were to be permanent, this process might take six months or longer) listening and sounding out workers.

Don't be shocked by the racist remarks of the white workers, by confused political impressions, by pro-war talk, by "keeping-up-with-the-Joneses" chit-chat. If the workers understood racism, the war, the capitalist class, middle class morality, etc., we'd be on the way "home" already. Do let them know you're a student fairly soon, within the first 2 or 3 weeks, as long as the foreman won't find out (or someone else who might use it to get you fired). But this isn't foolproof. You've got to play it by ear. But if you don't say you're a student, they'll know it and you won't be able to do an honest, straightforward job. Remember, although workers may think students are snobbish (and many are), they also respect education and want their kids to go to college. (That's why they're working so hard, among other reasons). Your job is to bring across the identity of interests of students and workers—the fact that without workers, there would be no universities, that the working class is the class with the power, that workers really create the value of society, that without them basic changes in the system can't happen, etc.

But you're there with a purpose—to bring out the relationship of the Vietnam and the other imperialist wars to their immediate demands, to the fact that they and their sons die in the war, that it is a war for the rich

—the class perspective. And also, among white workers, the use of racism against their other interests. Black workers aren't "threatening" their jobs. The boss is. He controls both. As long as workers are divided—by race, union, sex, craft, nationality, it's easier for the boss to sit on them. This is no easy task. It normally takes a lifetime, so don't expect to do it in two or three months! But at least you are able to question, to point out relationships they might not have thought of or might be afraid to express out loud. Try talking to workers individually, especially those who seem more receptive. Don't start by using a lunchroom or platform for a "soapbox oration". Literature could be given out individually or stuck up in bathrooms at the beginning. Discuss in your group when to start giving it out en masse (often by students not working at that plant, at the gates).

Try to make a few friends among the workers that might last beyond the summer. Two or three—or even one. And try to get their addresses and phone numbers before you leave the job. Otherwise it might be difficult to ever contact them again. Join the bowling league or the base-ball team. Avoid running home at the end of the day to the "safe" company of your old friends and political buddies. Concentrate on making new friends. Go to the bar or whatever hang-out they go to after work. Don't try to overdo yourself here. If you can't hold your liquor, don't make a fool of yourself trying to be what you think is "one of the boys". Get to work early—sit around and talk. This is very much worth the extra effort.

Don't talk to workers like you know everything and they know nothing. First of all it's not true (probably the reverse). Secondly, even if you do know more about a particular subject (i.e. the facts about the Geneva Agreement, the U.S. support of the Diem dictatorship) that doesn't mean that by making a speech you'll get the facts across. Be patient. Make it an exchange of experience, not a one-way affair. You'll make plenty of mistakes. Discuss them in your group. Don't give up the first time you do something wrong. After all, these workers were rookies too once, but they had to survive it because they had to eat.

It would be a good idea to record your experiences by day or week, a few notes in the evening about relevant events during the day will be invaluable for other people participating in the work-in this summer, for those in next summer's program and for people to whom we pub-licize our work. You'd be surprised how much important information you forget; don't trust to your chances of remembering anecdotes.

Come in to work on time! ! ! That's the thing that may keep you in the job above all else. Lateness is the first cause of being fired in the trial period. Don't start in with broadsides against the union leadership, even if workers initiate the sellout talk. Listen, ask questions, ask if anything was ever done to overcome it, suggest types of fights around grievances, immediate things, if you can figure some out. But don't feel compelled (in your three-month sojourn) to give leadership on any and all questions. One important result of your job may just be an appreciation of what workers are up against in the fight against the boss, the government, and a sellout leadership. And knowledge of what the in-plant grievances are will help if there is to be follow-up along lines of worker-student alliance activity when you get back to school. You will be able to relate leaflets, etc. to the actual problems inside the gates.

Lastly, remember when you start talking about the war (and about how students are seriously opposed to the war for good reasons, not simply engaged in "beatnik pranks") many workers who feel the same way keep silent while those who support the war are many times the most outspoken. Don't get into knock-down, drag-out arguments with the latter, but rather talk individually first to the ones you're making friends with. Don't get into the habit of making it appear that it's you against the workers. Know the facts about the war not just the polemics. Facts make a deep impression on workers. If you get involved in discussions with workers whose sons are in Vietnam and want to "support them by going all out" BE CAREFUL. That's an emotional area in which it may be very hard to convince such a father that your line on supporting his son is correct. Start by understanding his position of having been brainwashed all these years and seeing his son in daily danger of "being killed by the other side." In learning how to put forth an intelligent approach in such situations, you will really be learning how to talk to people who are not simply on your side or sympathetic.

After being there about a month, try to pick out a few workers who might be more advanced than the rest, concentrating more on individual discussion, with the hope of keeping them as friends or contacts after you leave the place. Talk about the possibilities of the students offering the workers assistance in any struggles coming up in the future, or picket lines, demonstrations, even doing research for them. Don't necessarily start asking about union meetings. Many times they are suspended in the summer. If not, most workers don't attend and you're not going to build up any active attitude caucus movement in that direction in three months (most of which is spent on trial period and during which you may not even be in the union). If, of course, there's something special going on and lots of workers appear headed toward a union meeting, you can go with them, but more to listen and learn than to orate.

Not everything can be put down here about what you'll face. Keep in constant contact with your group and discuss all problems with them. If possible, try to have at least two students (possibly more) get jobs in the same plant so they can compare notes, exchange experiences, criticize each other's mistakes, and (probably most important) make it possible to get a broader view of the place than that which comes from working in just one department. However, if you do team up, don't hang around together. It will be a constant temptation to talk to, eat and travel with the one person in your work-site who will be easier to communicate with. This is not to say that you should ignore each other's existence on the job, just that your primary aim will be to work and communicate with the permanent workers in the plant.

DOCUMENT No. 5

New Left "Counter-Orientation" Program

Leaders of the New Left kicked off the new school year in 1969 with week-long "counter-orientation" programs on various campuses of the country. These indicate the scope and character of the indoctrination work being conducted on college and university campuses by different radical groups, both white and black. An example of these programs is the one held at the University of North Carolina at Chapel Hill, reported as follows by *protean/RADISH*, a radical weekly, in its issue of September 15-21:

WEDNESDAY, SEPTEMBER 17

"The Black Liberation Struggle" 2:00 pm Room 111 Murphey Hall
    Films: Black Panther—the program of the Black Panther Party, interviews with Huey Newton and Eldridge Cleaver
                Mayday—Free Huey rally in Oakland, California, on Mayday. Panthers and others speak on the repression of the Black Liberation Struggle
  Speakers: Bobby Lee—Field Secretary for the Illinois Black Panther Party
             Adolph Reed—former UNC student
             Alex Willingham—UNC Political Science Graduate Student
"The White Revolutionary and Black Liberation" 7:30 pm Great Hall, CU
  Speakers: Bill Fesperman—Field Secretary of the Young Patriots
             Craig Walden—Minister of Defense of the Young Patriots (The Young Patriot Organization is a political organization of working youth of the Uptown area in Chicago. Many originally came from the South and Appalachia.)
"Black Liberation in North Carolina" 8:15 pm Great Hall, Carolina U.
  Speakers: Howard Fuller—North Carolina community organizer, formally with the North Carolina Fund, the Foundation for Community Development (FCD), and an instructor at UNC. Currently with the Malcolm X University in Durham.
             Chuck Hopkins—former leader of the Duke Afro-American Society and now with the Malcolm X University.
             Members of the Black Student Movement at UNC.

THURSDAY, SEPTEMBER 18   BUILDING A WORKING CLASS MOVEMENT
"Community and Factory Organizing" 4:00 Room 207, Carolina Union
   Panel: ACT staffer (ACT is a white community action organization
            in Durham.)
            Clint Pyne—(UNC student, member of the Carolina Summer
            Labor Project)
            Member of Hospital Workers Union, Local 1199 which has
            organized in the 4 Durham hospitals
"American Revolution II" 7:30 pm Great Hall, Carolina Union
   Film: American Revolution II—Black Panthers and Young Patriots
            organizing in Chicago, interviews with members of the
            poor white and black communities of Chicago; the 1968
            Democratic National Convention riots.
  Speakers: Bill Fesperman—Field Secretary of the Young Patriots
            Bobby Lee—Field Secretary of the Illinois Black Panthers
            Craig Walden—Minister of Defense of the Young Patriots

FRIDAY, SEPTEMBER 19   WOMEN'S LIBERATION
"An Introduction to Women's Liberation" 4:00 Room 207, Carolina Union
            (Meeting for Women Only)
"Women's Oppression and a History of Women's Liberation
            (Open Meeting) 7:30 pm Room 111 Murphey Hall

SUNDAY, SEPTEMBER 21   MARXISM
"Marxism and the U.S." 8:00 Room 207, Carolina Union
   Panel: Ed Lavalle—Duke Graduate Instructor, with the Student
            Liberation Front
            Nick Atkins—former union organizer, instructor in Russian
            at Duke—speaking on Marxism and workers movement
            Adolph Reed—former UNC student—speaking on Marxism
            and Black Liberation
            George Vlasits—former statewide SSOC organizer—speaking
            on Marxism and the Youth Movement

MONDAY, SEPTEMBER 22   IMPERIALISM
"Vietnam Will Win" 4:00 pm Room 207, Carolina Union
  Speaker: Carl Davidson—former national officer of SDS, currently with
            the *Guardian*, recently returned from Cuba where he
            met with workers, soldiers, students, and minority group
            members representing the Provisional Revolutionary Gov-
            ernment of South Vietnam.

"Imperialism: A Look at American Foreign Policy"
            7:30 Room 111 Murphey Hall
    Films: FALN—the Venezuela Liberation Movement
                Isle of Youth—a Cuban film presenting an alternative to a
                society dependent on racism and exploitation.
    Panel: Fred Bode—UNC history professor
                Larry Kessler—UNC history professor, specializing in Asia
                Carl Davidson—*Guardian* staffer—speaking on Latin America

TUESDAY, SEPTEMBER 23   YOUTH MOVEMENT
"Response to Repression" 4:00 Room 207, Carolina Union
    Panel: Clint Pyne—UNC student
                Jim Rowan Duke law students and organizers
                Buddy Tieger of the Southern Legal Action Movement
                (SLAM)
                Judy Weinberg—former UNC student
                Carl Davidson—*Guardian* staff
"Revolutionary Youth Movement" 7:30 pm Room 111 Murphey Hall
    Film: People's Park—the struggle of the Berkeley people to save
                the park.
    Panel: Mike Tola—former SSOC organizer, currently with the *Radish*
                Scott Bradley—*Radish* staff
                Meg Rose—formerly with YSA, currently with the *Radish*
                Dick Roman—Instructor, UNC Department of Sociology,
                Active in the Berkeley Free Speech Movement
                Jim Kahan—just back from France, former UNC graduate
                student
                Carl Davidson—*Guardian* staff

Index

PHOTO CREDITS

43-201